EXAM QUESTION PRACTICE PACK

AQA GCSE (9–1) COMPUTER SCIENCE

Every effort has been made to trace all copyright holders, but if any have been inadvertently overlooked, the Publishers will be pleased to make the necessary arrangements at the first opportunity.

Hachette UK's policy is to use papers that are natural, renewable and recyclable products and made from wood grown in well-managed forests and other controlled sources. The logging and manufacturing processes are expected to conform to the environmental regulations of the country of origin.

Orders: please contact Hachette UK Distribution, Hely Hutchinson Centre, Milton Road, Didcot, Oxfordshire, OX11 7HH. Telephone: (44) 01235 827827. Email education@hachette.co.uk Lines are open from 9 a.m. to 5 p.m., Monday to Friday. You can also order through our website: www.hoddereducation.co.uk

ISBN: 978 1 5104 3351 9

© Hodder & Stoughton 2018

First published in 2018 by
Hodder Education,
An Hachette UK Company
Carmelite House
50 Victoria Embankment
London EC4Y 0DZ

www.hoddereducation.co.uk

Impression number   10 9 8 7 6 5 4

Year   2022   2021

All rights reserved. Apart from any use permitted under UK copyright law, the material in this publication is copyright and cannot be photocopied or otherwise produced in its entirety or copied onto acetate without permission. Electronic copying is not permitted. Permission is given to teachers to make limited copies of pages 5–96, for classroom distribution only, to students within their own school or educational institution. The material may not be copied in full, in unlimited quantities, kept on behalf of others, distributed outside the purchasing institution, copied onwards, sold to third parties, or stored for future use in a retrieval system. This permission is subject to the payment of the purchase price of the book. If you wish to use the material in any way other than as specified, you must apply in writing to the Publisher at the above address.

Cover photo: Fotolia/Edelweiss

Typeset in India

Printed by Hobbs the Printers Ltd, Totton, Hampshire SO40 3WX

A catalogue record for this title is available from the British Library.

CONTENTS

Introduction 4

Exam questions 5

Paper 1 Computational thinking and problem solving 5
1.1 Fundamentals of algorithms 5
1.2 Programming 10
1.3 Fundamentals of data representation 13
1.4 Computer systems 17

Paper 2 Written assessment 21
2.1 Fundamentals of data representation 21
2.2 Computer systems 26
2.3 Fundamentals of computer networks 29
2.4 Fundamentals of cyber security 31
2.5 Ethical, legal and environmental impacts of digital technology 32

Example responses and mark schemes 34

Paper 1 Computational thinking and problem solving 34
1.1 Fundamentals of algorithms 34
1.2 Programming 44
1.3 Fundamentals of data representation 51
1.4 Computer systems 58

Paper 2 Written assessment 66
2.1 Fundamentals of data representation 66
2.2 Computer systems 77
2.3 Fundamentals of computer networks 85
2.4 Fundamentals of cyber security 89
2.5 Ethical, legal and environmental impacts of digital technology 93

The assessment objectives (AOs) 95
Breakdown of assessment objectives for GCSE 96

INTRODUCTION

This pack of exam-style questions, example responses and mark schemes is specially curated for the AQA GCSE (9–1) Computer Science specification. The pack is divided into two sections:

- **Exam questions**. A bank of questions similar to those found in AQA GCSE (9–1) Computer Science papers. These are arranged in the order of topics in the specification. You may wish to photocopy all or part of them for use with your class.
- **Example responses and mark schemes**. For each question there are two student responses — a 'Student A' response typical of an answer receiving a high mark, and a 'Student B' response that would receive fewer marks. Each response includes examiner-style commentary which describes why they receive the marks they do. The mark scheme for each question indicates how these responses could be graded, and can be used alongside each type of student answer or just with the question.

The pack is designed to help you to:
- encourage students to reflect on their responses and ensure they know how to succeed
- cultivate students' key skills and knowledge by regular assessment throughout the course, or in the revision period before the exams
- incorporate question practice into your lesson plans in the final, vital stage of teaching a topic: putting theory into practice
- teach flexibly, choosing photocopiable pages as appropriate to share with students
- facilitate peer discussion of what is good or better about given answers, which allows greater insight into quality responses
- allow students to analyse responses without the bias that can come from looking at their own or their friends' work — and so get more from the task

The assessment objectives (AOs)

The assessment objectives for AQA GCSE Computer Science are described, and their weightings explained, on page 95.

EXAM QUESTIONS

Paper 1 Computational thinking and problem solving

1.1 Fundamentals of algorithms

1   The design of algorithms is an important aspect of computer science.
   (a) Explain what is meant by the term 'algorithm'. (2 marks)

   (b) The design of an algorithm comes from the abstraction and decomposition of a given problem. Explain how both these methods are used to identify what algorithms should be designed so that a problem can be solved. (4 marks)

   (c) The pseudo code for a simple algorithm is outlined below:

   ```
   1  a ← USERINPUT
   2  b ← a * 2
   3  OUTPUT b
   ```

   Explain the steps in this algorithm. (2 marks)

Total: 8 marks

(Example student responses and mark scheme on p. 34)

2 An algorithm has been designed to control an automatic barrier on the entry to a car park.

(a) Shade three lozenges to identify the correct statements about a computer control system for a car park barrier similar to the one described above. **(3 marks)**

A The motor controlling the barrier is an output device for the system. ◯

B A car under the barrier is an output device for the system. ◯

C A proximity sensor to detect a car is an input device for the system. ◯

D A flashing error light on the console is an input device for the system. ◯

E Checking the number of cars in the car park is a processing task in the system. ◯

F Fixing paper jams on the ticket dispenser is a processing task in the system. ◯

(b) The following algorithm is used to track the number of cars in the car park (when full it holds 50 cars):

```
1  updateInputs()
2  WHILE (systemOn = True)
3    IF (carAtExit = True) THEN
4      WHILE (carAtExit ≠ False)
5        openExit()
6        updateInputs()
7      ENDWHILE
8      spaces = spaces - 1
9      closeExit()
10     ELSE IF (carAtEnt = True) AND (spaces < 50) THEN
11       ticketOut()
12       WHILE (carAtEnt ≠ False)
13         openEntrance()
14         updateInputs()
15       ENDWHILE
16       spaces = spaces + 1
17       closeEntrance()
18     ELSE IF (spaces = 50) THEN
19       carParkFull()
20     ENDIF
21  ENDWHILE
```

Note that the variables are global. The subroutine updateInputs() polls the physical sensors within the car park and updates the variables carAtExit, and carAtEnt and systemOn. For example, if a sensor detects there is a car at the exit barrier, the function will update the variable carAtExit to True. There are already 48 cars in the car park.

Complete the following trace table to show what happens when another three cars attempt to enter without any leaving (assuming the algorithm starts on line 3). **(5 marks)**

carAtExit	carAtEnt	spaces
FALSE	TRUE	48
	TRUE	

Total: 8 marks

(Example student responses and mark scheme on p. 36)

3 Searching for specific data is a task well suited to a computer. A binary search algorithm is outlined below. For this algorithm the first array index is 1.

```
1  data ← [1, 4, 9, 16, 25, 36, 49]
2  a ← 25
3  b ← 1
4  c ← 7
5  WHILE b ≠ c
6   mid ← (b + c) DIV 2
7    IF a ≤ data [mid] THEN
8     c ← mid
9    ELSE
10    b ← mid + 1
11   ENDIF
12 ENDWHILE
13 IF a = data [b] THEN
14   found ← true
15 ELSE
16   found ← false
17 ENDIF
```

(a) Complete the following trace table for the binary search algorithm. **(6 marks)**

a	b	c	mid	data[mid]	found

(b) Linear search is an alternative search algorithm that also finds specified data in a given data set. Generally, the algorithm takes longer to complete than binary search. Explain why linear search will be faster if the search value a is 1. **(2 marks)**

(c) The pseudo code has not been designed well for this type of algorithm. Identify two more suitable variable names to use within the program. **(2 marks)**

Total: 10 marks

(Example student responses and mark scheme on p. 38)

4   A bubble sort algorithm can organise data in an array by comparing adjacent values and swapping them if they are out of order. This continues until the array is sorted and can require many passes.

(a) Data to be sorted are stored in an array, as shown below:

| 1 | 7 | 3 | 2 | 4 |

Complete the following diagram, showing the order of the data after every pass when sorted using a bubble sort. **(2 marks)**

Start	1	7	3	2	4
Pass 1					
Pass 2					

(b) Bubble sort requires a final pass through the array of data. Explain why this is necessary. **(2 marks)**

(c) The time taken for a bubble sort to completely sort an array of data is poor when all the values in the array are reversed. Merge sort improves on this, as it decomposes the task into several smaller, easier-to-solve tasks. Explain how merge sort does this. **(3 marks)**

Total: 7 marks

(Example student responses and mark scheme on p. 39)

5   A programmer is planning an algorithm to control a small motorised robot to navigate a maze such as the one shown in Figure 1.

Figure 1

(a) The programmer designs an algorithm whereby the robot always turns left when presented with a choice of paths. Complete the following flowchart so that the algorithm will work. **(2 marks)**

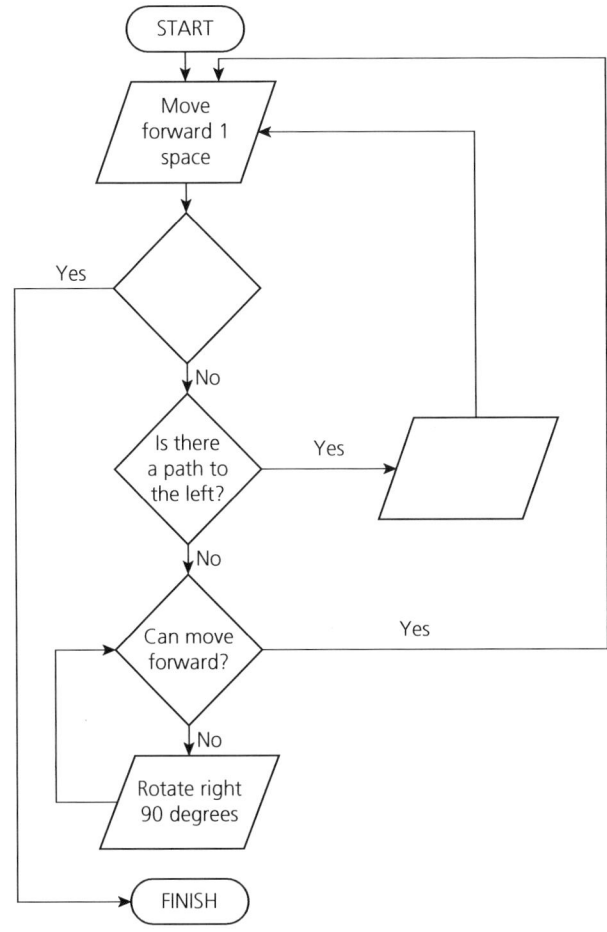

(b) Mark the route the robot would take along the maze according to the flowchart of the algorithm. **(4 marks)**

(c) How could this algorithm be modified to arrive at the end square more quickly? (The robot cannot move more than one square or 90° in one instruction.) **(1 mark)**

....

....

Total: 7 marks

(Example student responses and mark scheme on p. 41)

1.2 Programming

6 Computer programs store the data they use in variables.

(a) A program created to track book loans in a library uses the line of code shown below. Describe what the statement does. **(2 marks)**

```
booksLoaned ← 0
```

....

....

(b) The data type of the variable will be an Integer. Identify another numerical data type that could be used to store the same data and explain how it is different from an Integer. **(3 marks)**

....

....

(c) The total number of books that can be loaned at any one time is eight. Complete the code below to ensure that no more than eight books can be loaned. **(3 marks)**

```
booksLoaned ← 0
_ _ _ _ _ _ _ _ _ _ _ _ _ _ _ _ _ _
    INPUT userChoice
    IF userChoice = "loan" THEN
        booksLoaned ← _ _ _ _ _ _ _ _ _ _ _ _ _ _ _ _ _ _
    ENDIF
UNTIL _ _ _ _ _ _ _ _ _ _ _ _ _ _ _ _ _ _ OR userChoice = "finish"
```

Total: 8 marks

(Example student responses and mark scheme on p. 44)

7 (a) The line of code shown below is part of software used in a bank's cash point machine that dispenses only £10 notes. This ensures that the maximum withdrawal amount is the balance rounded down to the nearest £10. Explain how the DIV operator is used to round the maxWithdrawal amount to the nearest £10. **(3 marks)**

```
maxWithdrawal ← balance DIV 10
```

....

....

....

(b) Another part of the program ensures that the balance has to be in credit (above £0) before money can be withdrawn. This is coded as shown below. Explain why this does not work if the balance is overdrawn (i.e. the balance is a negative value). **(3 marks)**

```
IF (balance DIV 10 = 0) THEN
    OUTPUT "Withdrawal not allowed"
ELSE
    OUTPUT "Maximum withdrawal is"
    OUTPUT balance DIV 10
ENDIF
```

(c) Another part of the program ensures that the balance has to be in credit (above £0) before money can be withdrawn. This is coded as shown below. Explain how the condition of the IF statement can be modified so that the only withdrawal amounts allowed are multiples of 10 between (and including) £10 and £100. **(3 marks)**

```
IF (balance DIV 10 = 0) THEN
    OUTPUT "Withdrawal not allowed"
ELSE
    OUTPUT "Maximum withdrawal is"
    OUTPUT balance DIV 10
ENDIF
```

Total: 9 marks

(Example student responses and mark scheme on p. 45)

8 Modularised programming is a design technique where code is separated into subroutines.

   (a) Explain what a subroutine is. **(2 marks)**

   (b) Two subroutines have been created to generate a random password for new employees joining a company. The first takes the username as a parameter and returns the first three letters combined with the length of the username (see below).

```
SUBROUTINE
letters(user)
firstPart ← SUBSTRING(0, 3, user)
secondPart ← LEN(user)
return firstPart + INT_TO_STRING(secondPart)
ENDSUBROUTINE
```

   The second takes the username as a parameter and returns a random three-digit value added to the length of the username (see below).

```
SUBROUTINE
numbers(user)
firstNum ← RANDOM_INT(100, 999)
secondNum ← LEN(user)
return firstNum + secondNum
ENDSUBROUTINE
```

   Complete the code for the calling program that would create a string password and output on the screen:

```
username ← USERINPUT
```

   (5 marks)

(c) Describe two advantages of modularised programming for this solution. (4 marks)

Total: 11 marks

(Example student responses and mark scheme on p. 46)

9 Data are often collated together in data structures such as arrays.
   (a) Explain why an array is useful for storing a collection of five test scores that are expressed as integers. (2 marks)

   (b) The array is named testScores and has been populated with five integer scores ranging from 0 to 100. Create an algorithm, using a WHILE loop, that can find the average of these values. Assume that the first index of the array is 0. (4 marks)

Total: 6 marks

(Example student responses and mark scheme on p. 48)

10 Programming languages can be classified as either high level or low level.
  (a) Explain the advantages that high-level languages have over low-level languages when creating computer programs. **(4 marks)**

  (b) High-level languages can be converted to machine code using either an interpreter or a compiler. Explain how these two translators are different. **(2 marks)**

Total: 6 marks

(Example student responses and mark scheme on p. 49)

1.3 Fundamentals of data representation

11 There are many different ways to count. For example, the decimal system uses the symbols 0 to 9 to count objects in groups of 10. The decimal system is therefore referred to as base-10.
  (a) The binary number system is referred to as base-2. Explain how this is different from the decimal number system. **(2 marks)**

(b) The decimal value 250 is represented within a computer as an 8-bit binary byte. Complete the following table to show the value of each bit of the byte and the place values they represent. **(2 marks)**

Place value	128							1
Byte								

(c) The hexadecimal number system is considered as base-16. Explain why it is used in computer science, using the example binary value 11010011. **(4 marks)**

....

....

....

....

Total: 8 marks

(Example student responses and mark scheme on p. 51)

12 Computers are calculating devices. They complete actions based on the results of these calculations.

(a) Addition is a fundamental operation of computer processing. Add the following binary bytes (show your working). **(3 marks)**

10000010
00000101
00010100

....

....

....

....

(b) Bit shifting is another fundamental operation of a computer. With the example of the value 010, describe the two ways in which a binary value can be bit shifted and explain what each of these operations has the effect of doing to the value each time. **(4 marks)**

....

....

....

....

(c) A computer program has been written to determine the radioactivity of a sample of a material. The starting value of the number of billions of atoms within the sample is recorded as an 8-bit binary byte, for example 160 billion atoms would be stored as 10100000.

Half-life is a measurement of how long it takes for half the number of atoms in the sample to decay. For example, after one half-life the number of atoms in the example would be 80 billion, after a second half-life 40 billion, and so on.

Explain how bit-shifting can be used to track the number of atoms represented by an input number of half-lives. **(3 marks)**

....

....

....

....

Total: 10 marks

(Example student responses and mark scheme on p. 52)

13 A digital recording device is capturing the music played by an orchestra.
   (a) Explain how analogue sound waves can be represented as digital data using this device. **(2 marks)**

....

....

   (b) Twenty seconds of audio are sampled at 10,000 Hz with an 8-bit resolution. Calculate the file size in kB. Show your working and identify the original calculation used. **(4 marks)**

....

....

....

....

....

(c) Photos are taken on a digital camera and stored as bitmap images. Using the terms 'pixels' and 'colour depth', describe how the image is represented in binary. **(3 marks)**

....

....

....

(d) A 4-bit colour depth image is created with a 600-pixel width and 300-pixel length. Calculate the file size in bytes (show your working). **(2 marks)**

....

....

....

Total: 11 marks

(Example student responses and mark scheme on p. 54)

14 Data used by computer systems are often compressed to reduce the storage space required.

(a) An attachment sent with an email has been compressed by the sender. Explain two reasons why the user might have done this, in terms of reducing the overall size of the files being sent. **(4 marks)**

....

....

....

....

(b) Data can be compressed using a technique known as Huffman coding. A text file containing a sequence of six letters has been coded using the tree shown in Figure 2. The letter C would be coded as 100 (starting from the top requires one right move followed by two left moves to get to the letter). State the code for the following letters: A, D and F. **(3 marks)**

Figure 2

(c) Another method of compression is run length encoding (RLE). A file contains the following sequence of characters: AAAAABBBAAAAAADDDDDFFFFFFFFFFEEE. Using this example, explain what RLE is and how it could be used to reduce the sequence of characters shown. **(3 marks)**

Total: 10 marks

(Example student responses and mark scheme on p. 56)

1.4 Computer systems

15 Computer systems are the combination of hardware and software.
   (a) Describe how logic gates are used in a computer system. **(2 marks)**

   (b) A logic circuit is designed as shown in Figure 3. Complete the following truth table. **(4 marks)**

Figure 3

A	B	C	Q
0	0	0	1
0	0	1	0
0	1	0	1
0	1	1	0
1	0	0	
1	0	1	
1	1	0	
1	1	1	

(c) Logic gates are combined to create the circuitry required for memory. This is managed by an operating system (OS). Describe how an OS manages the following:
- I/O devices
- security
- processor

(3 marks)

Total: 9 marks

(Example student responses and mark scheme on p. 58)

16 Computers follow instructions within programs to process data into useful results.

(a) The Von Neumann architecture is a way of arranging a computer to process data from given instructions. Explain how data and instructions are stored and processed in a Von Neumann machine. (3 marks)

(b) Processors consist of two main components: the arithmetic logic unit (ALU) and the control unit. Explain the role of the ALU in completing program instructions. (2 marks)

(c) The fetch-execute cycle is used to coordinate all components of a processor to complete execution of a program. Describe the three stages of this cycle to explain how the processor produces a required output for a given instruction. **(3 marks)**

Total: 8 marks

(Example student responses and mark scheme on p. 60)

17 There are a variety of places where data are stored in a computer system.

(a) Secondary storage is considered a non-volatile data storage location. Explain this term and contrast it with volatile storage, giving an example. **(3 marks)**

(b) Secondary storage can be classified by three different types. The most common of these is magnetic, which stores data on metal by magnetising it in different patterns. Identify the other two methods of secondary storage and explain how they work. **(4 marks)**

(c) To supplement local storage, cloud storage is used as an alternative means of saving data for later use. Define the term 'cloud storage' and explain a benefit of using it to store files. **(3 marks)**

Total: 10 marks

(Example student responses and mark scheme on p. 62)

18 The performance of a computer system is affected by many different factors.

(a) The processor is a key component in determining overall system performance. Cache memory is included to improve performance. Explain how different cache types and sizes affect the performance of a processor. **(3 marks)**

(b) Processor performance is also affected by its clock speed and the number of cores. Explore how variations in these two factors affect the performance of a processor. **(4 marks)**

(c) System software can be used to improve the performance of a computer system. Explain how system software is different from application software, giving an example of how it can be used to improve performance. **(3 marks)**

Total: 10 marks

(Example student responses and mark scheme on p. 64)

Paper 2 Written assessment

2.1 Fundamentals of data representation

1   (a) Shade one lozenge to identify the hexadecimal number base. **(1 mark)**
    2   ◯
    10 ◯
    16 ◯

   (b) Convert the following bit pattern into decimal:
       10011010 **(1 mark)**

   (c) Convert the decimal number 96 to 8-bit binary. **(1 mark)**

   (d) Convert the hexadecimal number F2 to decimal. **(1 mark)**

   (e) State the largest and smallest numbers that can be stored in a byte. **(2 marks)**

   (f) A number of data units are given below. Shade one lozenge to identify the largest unit. **(1 mark)**
       3 GB   ◯
       2000 kB   ◯
       3001 MB   ◯

Total: 7 marks

(Example student responses and mark scheme on p. 66)

2   A photograph is taken using a digital camera and stored as an image file.
   (a) Explain how binary is used to represent the photograph. **(3 marks)**

(b) The image was taken with a 24-bit colour depth. Explain what is meant by a 24-bit colour depth. **(2 marks)**

(c) The colour depth of the image is decreased to 8 bits. Explain two effects this will have on the image file. **(4 marks)**

(d) A 5 pixel by 5 pixel black and white image has the following data:
1 0 0 0 0 1 0 1 1 1 1 0 1 0 1 1 0 1 0 1 1 1 1 0 0
and uses the rule 1 = black, 0 = white.
Convert the given data into an image. **(5 marks)**

Total: 14 marks

(Example student responses and mark scheme on p. 68)

3 (a) Add together the following binary numbers, showing your working. (2 marks)
       0 0 1 0 1 1 1 0
       1 0 1 1 1 1 0 1

   (b) Add together the following binary numbers, showing your working. (3 marks)
       0 0 0 0 0 1 1 0
       1 0 1 0 1 1 0 1
       0 0 1 0 0 1 1 0

   (c) Perform a 2-place logical right shift on the binary number 01100100, giving your answer as an 8-bit binary number. (1 mark)

   (d) Perform a 3-place logical left shift on the binary number 01101011, giving your answer as an 11-bit number. (1 mark)

   (e) Describe the effect of performing a 2-place left shift on a binary number. (2 marks)

   (f) Describe the effect of performing a 3-place right shift on a binary number. (2 marks)

Total: 11 marks

(Example student responses and mark scheme on p. 70)

4 Text is stored in a file.

(a) Explain what is meant by a character set. (2 marks)

(b) Describe the difference between ASCII and Unicode. (2 marks)

(c) Describe one benefit and one drawback of using the character set Unicode instead of ASCII to store a text file. (4 marks)

(d) Part of a character set is shown in the table below. State the binary code for J. (1 mark)

A	01000001
B	01000010
C	01000011
D	01000100
E	01000101

(e) A computer program takes a UK postcode as input, which is compared to the postcodes stored in the program. Explain why the postcode is case sensitive. (3 marks)

Total: 12 marks

(Example student responses and mark scheme on p. 72)

5   A video camera is being used to record a music video. The video file is compressed when stored on a computer.

(a) Describe how analogue waves are recorded and stored on the camera. (3 marks)

(b) Define the term 'sample resolution'. (1 mark)

(c) Define the term 'sample rate'. (1 mark)

(d) Give the formula for estimating the size of a sound file. (2 marks)

(e) The visual part of the video is made up of many frames. Each frame is a single bitmap image. Each image is 1000 pixels by 500 pixels. The colour depth is 8 bytes. Estimate the file size of one frame in MB. (4 marks)

(f) State the purpose of file compression. (1 mark)

(g) Explain, using an example, how run length encoding (RLE) can be used to compress a single frame of the video image. (3 marks)

Total: 15 marks

(Example student responses and mark scheme on p. 74)

2.2 Computer systems

6 A logic circuit is: A AND NOT (B OR C).

(a) Create a logic circuit diagram for the logic circuit given above. (3 marks)

(b) Complete the following truth table for the logic circuit given above. (4 marks)

A	B	C	NOT (B OR C)	Output
0	0	0		
0	0	1		
0	1	0		
0	1	1		
1	0	0		
1	0	1		
1	1	0		
1	1	1		

(c) Write the logic circuit for the logic circuit diagram shown in Figure 1. (3 marks)

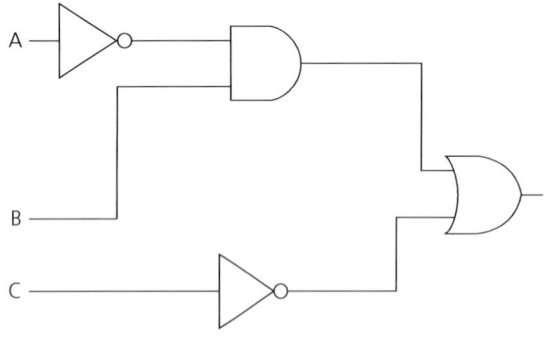

Figure 1

Total: 10 marks

(Example student responses and mark scheme on p. 77)

7 Lewis has purchased a laptop to replace his slow-running PC. The laptop comes with system software and application software.

(a) Explain the difference between system software and application software. **(2 marks)**

(b) Give two examples of system software and two examples of application software. **(4 marks)**

(c) Lewis could have upgraded his previous PC instead of buying a new laptop. Identify two ways Lewis could have upgraded his PC, explaining the effect each would have had on the CPU. **(6 marks)**

Total: 12 marks

(Example student responses and mark scheme on p. 79)

8 A computer has been purchased with an operating system and utility programs pre-installed.

(a) One example of a utility program is defragmentation. Describe two additional utility programs that may have come with the computer. **(4 marks)**

(b) Explain the need for and functions of an operating system. (8 marks)

Total: 12 marks

(Example student responses and mark scheme on p. 81)

9   A computer uses Von Neumann architecture. The CPU is a key component of Von Neumann architecture.

  (a) Using an example, state the role(s) of the arithmetic logic unit (ALU) in a CPU. (3 marks)

  (b) Describe the role of the control unit in a CPU. (2 marks)

  (c) Explain the role of the clock in a CPU. (3 marks)

Total: 8 marks

(Example student responses and mark scheme on p. 83)

2.3 Fundamentals of computer networks

10 A small business that employs 20 staff in a single building is setting up a computer network.
   (a) Explain whether the business should set up a LAN or a WAN, giving reasons for
       your choice. (4 marks)

   (b) The business will also make use of PANs (Personal Area Networks). Give two examples of
       PANs that the business may have and a different example of what it is used for. (4 marks)

   (c) Two common network protocols are TCP (Transmission Control Protocol) and IP (Internet
       Protocol). Identify two additional network protocols and explain their purpose. (6 marks)

Total: 14 marks

(Example student responses and mark scheme on p. 85)

11 Harrison is connecting his business LAN to the internet. A range of protocols is used to transmit data on the internet.

(a) State what is meant by a protocol. **(1 mark)**

....

(b) Name two different email protocols. **(2 marks)**

....

(c) TCP is made up of layers. The table below has two layers already written in. Write the names of the other two layers in the correct places. **(2 marks)**

| Application |
| Transport |
| |
| |

(d) Using an example, explain the purpose of the transport layer. **(2 marks)**

....

....

....

....

(e) Harrison enters a URL to view his company's website. Explain how IP addresses are used to view the website. **(4 marks)**

....

....

....

....

....

....

....

Total: 11 marks

(Example student responses and mark scheme on p. 87)

2.4 Fundamentals of cyber security

12 JLRS is a nationwide bank that is concerned about cyber security threats to its data.

(a) Explain what is meant by cyber security. **(2 marks)**

(b) One cyber security threat is malicious code. Using examples, describe two other cyber security threats and the dangers they pose to the bank and its customers. **(8 marks)**

(c) JLRS employs an external company to perform penetration testing on the bank's website. Explain what is meant by penetration testing and how it will be used on the bank's website. **(5 marks)**

(d) The bank allows new customers to sign up online. It is worried about bots applying for and setting up fake accounts. Describe two authentication methods that could be used to check that the customer wanting to set up the account is real. **(6 marks)**

....

....

....

....

....

....

Total: 21 marks

(Example student responses and mark scheme on p. 89)

13 (a) Shade two lozenges to identify the two examples of malware. **(2 marks)**

- Virus ⚬
- Hacker ⚬
- Pharming ⚬
- Trojan ⚬
- Phishing ⚬

(b) Name one additional piece of malware not given in part (a). **(1 mark)**

....

Total: 3 marks

(Example student responses and mark scheme on p. 92)

2.5 Ethical, legal and environmental impacts of digital technology

14 Technology is becoming smaller and more wearable, for example the introduction of smart watches and fitness trackers. Discuss the advantages and disadvantages of wearable technology. In your answer, you should consider any legal, social and environmental issues related to the technologies. **(9 marks)**

....

....

....

....

Total: 9 marks

(Example student responses and mark scheme on p. 93)

EXAMPLE RESPONSES AND MARK SCHEMES

The student responses

This section shows sample answers from two students. One set (A) is strong, the other (B) weaker. The answers are followed by expert comments (shown by the icon 🅔) that indicate where credit is due. In the weaker answers, they also point out areas for improvement, specific problems and common errors.

Paper 1 Computational thinking and problem solving

1.1 Fundamentals of algorithms

Example responses

Question 1
Student A

(a) An algorithm is an ordered set of instructions that, when followed, carries out a task that needs to be performed.

🅔 **1 mark for identifying that it consists of instructions. 1 mark for confirming that following the steps completes the task that the algorithm was designed to complete. 2 marks**

(b) The process of abstraction allows an algorithm designer to focus on the important parts of the problem, removing the parts that are unimportant and that might make finding the solution more difficult. Decomposition is breaking a problem apart into smaller sub-tasks, which is helpful for the designer.

🅔 **1 mark for explaining the removal of unrequired information about the problem, 1 mark for explaining that the solution is not as obvious with too much unnecessary information. 1 mark for explaining that decomposition is the breaking apart of a problem, but no second mark as the benefit hasn't been explained. 3 marks**

(c) The algorithm works by reading an inputted value provided by the user and the value doubled is output.

🅔 **1 mark for identifying that input takes place, 1 mark for recognising that the input value is doubled and output. 2 marks**

> **Question 1**
> Student B
>
> (a) An algorithm is a sequence that produces some output or action to solve a problem.
>
> ⓔ It is not clear what a sequence actually is, so no mark is awarded. 1 mark for identifying that an algorithm produces a solution to a problem. **1 mark**
>
> (b) Abstraction is where simplifications are created for what you are designing. Decomposition is splitting a problem apart to smaller ones.
>
> ⓔ For abstraction, the mark is not awarded as it is not clear what simplification means in this context. For decomposition, 1 mark is awarded for explaining the breaking apart of a problem, but no second mark is gained for explaining the benefit of doing so. **1 mark**
>
> (c) The algorithm works by multiplying an input by two.
>
> ⓔ 1 mark for correctly identifying the process of the algorithm, but the student is not clear about input and/or output. **1 mark**

Question 1 mark scheme

(a) 1 mark for each of the following points:
- A sequence of steps/instructions…
- …that, when followed, completes a task.

(b) 1 mark for each of the following points about abstraction:
- Removing all the unnecessary information about the problem so that only the important aspects of the problem remain…
- …making the design of the solution clearer.

1 mark for each of the following points about decomposition:
- Breaking down a single large problem into several smaller parts…
- …so that each part is easier to design compared to the whole.

(c) 2 marks from:
- User inputs a value of their choice.
- Input is doubled.
- Doubled value is output.

Question 2
Student A

(a)
A The motor controlling the barrier is an output device for the system. ●
B A car under the barrier is an output device for the system. ○
C A proximity sensor to detect a car is an input device for the system. ●
D A flashing error light on the console is an input device for the system. ○
E Checking the number of cars in the car park is a processing task in the system. ●
F Fixing paper jams on the ticket dispenser is a processing task in the system. ○

⊙ 1 mark for the system signals the motor to open or close the gate. 1 mark for cars need to be detected by the system. 1 mark for this will be tracked by the number of times the barrier opens and the position of the cars when it does. **3 marks**

(b)

carAtEx	t carAtEnt	spaces
FALSE	TRUE	48
	FALSE	
		49
	TRUE	
	FALSE	
		50
	TRUE	

⊙ FALSE = 1 mark — holds until car moves through; 49 = 1 mark — count updated; TRUE = 1 mark — next car arrives; FALSE = 1 mark — holds until car goes through; 50 = 1 mark — count updated. **5 marks**

Question 2
Student B

(a)
A The motor controlling the barrier is an output device for the system. ●
B A car under the barrier is an output device for the system. ●
C A proximity sensor to detect a car is an input device for the system. ○
D A flashing error light on the console is an input device for the system. ●
E Checking the number of cars in the car park is a processing task in the system. ○
F Fixing paper jams on the ticket dispenser is a processing task in the system. ○

(e) 1 mark for the system signals the motor to open or close the gate. The car is not part of the system. Light is an output device. **1 mark**

(b)

carAtExit	carAtEnt	spaces
FALSE	TRUE	48
		49
	FALSE	
	TRUE	
	FALSE	
		49
	TRUE	

(e) 49 = no mark — out of order as count adjusted after car drives through; FALSE = no mark — car drives off before changing the count; TRUE = 1 mark — next car arrives; FALSE = 1 mark — holds until car goes through; 49 = no mark — count not updated. **2 marks**

Question 2 mark scheme

(a) 1 mark for each correctly shaded lozenge.
 A The motor controlling the barrier is an output device for the system. ●
 B A car under the barrier is an output device for the system. ○
 C A proximity sensor to detect a car is an input device for the system. ●
 D A flashing error light on the console is an input device for the system. ○
 E Checking the number of cars in the car park is a processing task in the system. ●
 F Fixing paper jams on the ticket dispenser is a processing task in the system. ○

(b) 1 mark for correct entry.

carAtExit	carAtEnt	spaces
FALSE	TRUE	48
	FALSE	
		49
	TRUE	
	FALSE	
		50
	TRUE	

Question 3

Student A

(a)

a	b	c	mid	data[mid]	found
25	1	7	4	16	
	5	6	6	36	
		5	5	25	true

The values in all six columns are correct. 6 marks

(b) As the target datum is at the start of the array, and linear search would start from this position, the datum would be found straight away. Binary search starts in the middle of the array and would therefore take longer to reach the target value as it has to narrow down the search range each time.

Linear search looks at the start of the array and the datum is there, so no further comparisons are required (1). Binary search always starts in the middle, so if the datum is found at the ends of the array the search will take longer (1). 2 marks

(c) a = val b = left

1 mark for a — indicates that a value needs to be found. 1 mark for b — indicates that the value represents the left portion of the array to search from. 2 marks

Question 3

Student B

(a)

a	b	c	mid	data[mid]	found
25	1	7	4	16	
	5	6	6	36	
				25	false

2 marks for the correct values in the first two columns. In the third column, no marks are awarded as the last step does not consider that the end value is required. The sequence needs to be checked carefully. The same is true for the fourth column — no marks are awarded. 1 mark for the correct values in the fifth column, but in the last column no marks are awarded — the student has not considered the last update of c and mid, therefore this output is wrong. Values of variables should be checked carefully. 3 marks

(b) Linear search will always be quicker because the datum you are looking for is at the front of the array so the search will find it first.

1 mark for explaining why linear search finds the datum quickly. However, to get the second mark the answer needs to compare this performance against binary search. 1 mark

(c) a = number b = leftPos

No mark for a — still too generic. Variables need to give an indication as to the data that will be stored in them. 1 mark for b — indicates that the value represents the left portion of the array to search from. 1 mark

Question 3 mark scheme

(a) 1 mark for each correct column.

a	b	c	mid	data[mid]	found
25	1	7	4	16	
	5	6	6	36	
		5	5	25	true

(b) 1 mark for each of the following points:
- Linear search in this case would find the value at the first attempt.
- Binary search would have to narrow down the result each time, having started in the middle of the array.

(c) 1 mark for each point or suitable alternative (2 max.):
- a — value
- b — left
- c — right

Question 4
Student A

(a)

Start	1	7	3	2	4
Pass 1	1	3	2	4	7
Pass 2	1	2	3	4	7

Both passes are correct. **2 marks**

(b) Bubble sort requires a final pass through to check the data are in the correct order. If it passes through and there is a swap, this indicates the data still might be out of order and need to be checked again.

First sentence, 1 mark — the student has identified the data are in order if no swaps detected. Second sentence, 1 mark — the repetitive nature of the algorithm detects swaps have taken place and continues checking if swaps have been required on the previous pass. **2 marks**

(c) Merge sort takes the set of data and splits it into two equal parts. Each of these equal parts is split again and again until the data of each sub-list are in order. These smaller lists are joined back together in order, so that the data are reconstructed in the correct sequence and the data are sorted

1 mark for data initially split. 1 mark for data continue to be split until each small list is in order. 1 mark for lists are recombined so that the data are reordered completely. **3 marks**

Question 4
Student B

(a)
Start	1	7	3	2	4
Pass 1	1	3	7	2	4
Pass 2	1	3	2	7	4

- **e** Both passes are incorrect; the student has made one move instead of making an entire pass through the array. No marks are awarded

(b) Bubble sort does a last pass through the data so that it can tell the data are in the correct order.

- **e** The student has indicated that a final pass is required to check the order (1), but is not clear about the fact that the algorithm repeats passes based on previous exchanges. **1 mark**

(c) Merge sort allows the data to be broken apart. They are then repeatedly broken apart until the values are in the correct order.

- **e** 1 mark for data initially split. 1 mark for identifying that the splitting of data continues until each subset is in order. The final mark is not awarded as the student hasn't explained that the solutions are recombined. **2 marks**

Question 4 mark scheme

(a) 1 mark for each correct row (pass 1 and pass 2 only):

Start	1	7	3	2	4
Pass 1	1	3	2	4	7
Pass 2	1	2	3	4	4

(b) 1 mark for each of the following points:
- The algorithm repeats if any data is swapped when passing through.
- The last pass with no swaps indicates the data are in order.

(c) 1 mark for the following points (max. 3 marks):
- Array of data is split into two.
- Each sub-list is split again until it is separate elements.
- Take adjacent pairs of two elements and merge them to form a list of two elements.
- Repeat the process of merging until you have a single sorted list.

Question 5
Student A

(a)

[Flowchart: START → Move forward 1 space → decision (Yes loops to left path / No continues) → "Is there a path to the left?" (Yes → blank parallelogram; No → continues) → "Can move forward?" (Yes → back to Move forward 1 space; No → Rotate right 90 degrees → loops back) → FINISH]

- e 1 mark for 'End found?' 1 mark for turn left when path found. **2 marks**

(b)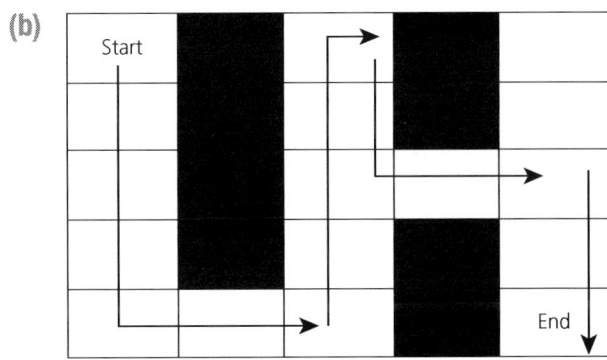

- e All parts of the path are correct. **4 marks**

(c) If the robot was told to turn right wherever possible it would get to the end sooner and would not go down the dead-ends.

- e The algorithm modified to turn right instead of left would reach the destination sooner. **1 mark**

Question 5
Student B

(a)

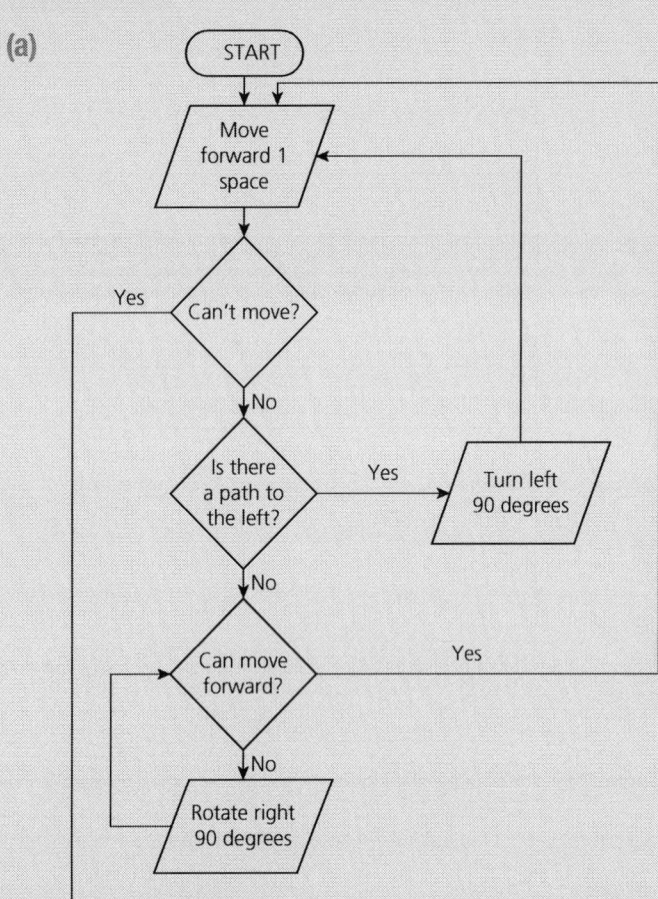

ⓔ No mark for 'Can't move?' as this is already dealt with later in the algorithm. 1 mark for 'Turn left 90 degrees'.

(b)

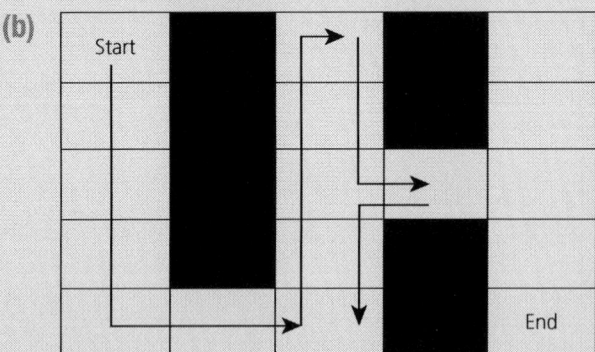

ⓔ 1 mark — first left turn correct; 1 mark — turn at dead-end and then left correct. No other marks are awarded as the robot then returns to Start. **2 marks**

(c) The robot could be told to keep going forward until it reaches a dead-end, then try and turn left.

ⓔ **The robot would still go to end of routes and delay reaching the end point, so no mark is awarded.**

Question 5 mark scheme

(a) 1 mark for each similarly worded instruction.

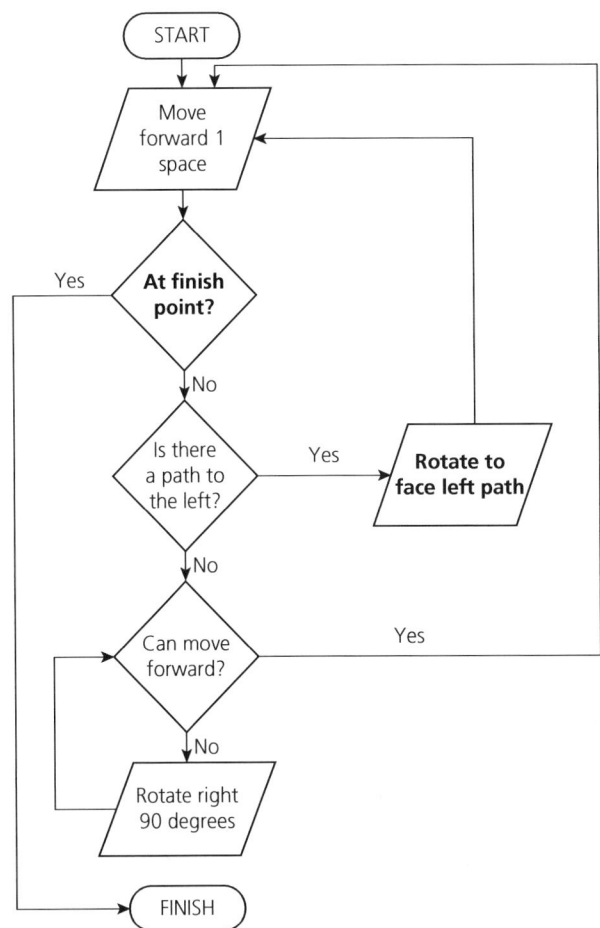

(b) 1 mark for each part of the route correctly identified.

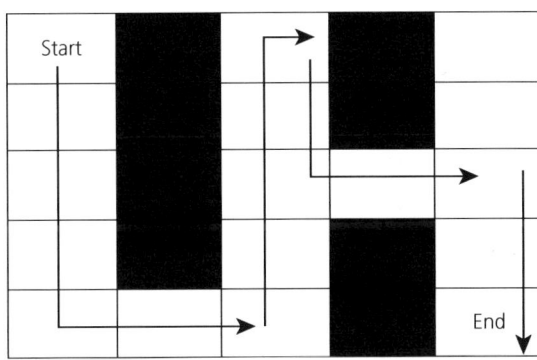

(c) 1 mark for 'Switch the turn direction throughout the algorithm (i.e. turns right instead of left and left instead of right)'.

1.2 Programming

Question 6
Student A

(a) The value 0 is assigned to the variable booksLoaned.

e **1 mark for identifying the assignment, 1 mark for identifying the variable. 2 marks**

(b) The Real data type could be used. Reals are able to store numbers with fractions but Integers only store whole numbers.

e **1 mark for the correct data type, 1 mark for identifying Real as floating point, 1 mark for correct comparison. 3 marks**

(c)
```
booksLoaned ← 0
REPEAT
   INPUT userChoice
   IF userChoice = "loan" THEN
      booksLoaned ← booksLoaned + 1
   ENDIF
UNTIL booksLoaned => 8 OR userChoice = "finish"
```

e **1 mark for the correct loop, 1 mark for booksLoaned + 1 and 1 mark for the final line, which is allowed because it will work even though the > is unnecessary. 3 marks**

Question 6
Student B

(a) The variable booksLoaned is receiving and storing 0.

e **1 mark for identifying the variable, but no second mark is awarded as the student has not used the correct terminology. 1 mark**

(b) The Real data type could be used and it can store negative numbers but an Integer can't.

e **1 mark for the correct data type. No further marks are awarded as Integer can store negative numbers, so the difference described is incorrect. 1 mark**

(c)
```
booksLoaned ← 0
WHILE
   INPUT userChoice
   IF userChoice = "loan" THEN
      booksLoaned ← booksLoaned + 1
   ENDIF
UNTIL booksLoaned > 8 OR userChoice = "finish"
```

e **No mark for the incorrect loop, 1 mark for booksLoaned + 1, no mark for the final line as the loop only stops if the number of loans is greater than 8. 1 mark**

Question 6 mark scheme

(a) 1 mark for each of the following points
  - Variable named booksLoaned.
  - Value 0 assigned.

(b) 1 mark for each of the following points:
  - Real/Single/Double data type.
  - Real stores numbers with decimal point/fractions.
  - Integer stores whole numbers only.

(c) 1 mark for each entry completed correctly.
```
booksLoaned ← 0
REPEAT
  INPUT userChoice
  IF userChoice = "loan" THEN
    booksLoaned ← booksLoaned + 1
  ENDIF
UNTIL booksLoaned = 8 OR userChoice = "finish"
```

Question 7
Student A

(a) DIV is used to divide the balance by 10. The way that DIV works means that any remainder is removed. As it is divided by 10, this ensures that the answer is always a multiple of 10.

ⓔ 1 mark for the first sentence, 1 mark for the second, 1 mark for the third. **3 marks**

(b) If a negative balance is divided by 10, it will give a negative value. This will mean the IF statement will be false, meaning the negative withdrawal amount will be output.

ⓔ 1 mark for the first sentence, 1 mark for IF will be false, 1 mark for the final sentence. **3 marks**

(c) IF (balance DIV 10 > 0) AND (balance DIV 10 <= 10) THEN

ⓔ 1 mark for the first comparison, 1 mark for AND, 1 mark for the second comparison. **3 marks**

Question 7
Student B

(a) DIV is used to divide the value by 10. This rounds the balance to the nearest multiple of 10.

ⓔ 1 mark for the first sentence, but no marks for second as DIV does not round but removes any fractional part. **1 mark**

(b) Even negative numbers divided by 10 will give values that are not 0. This means that the program will sense that negatives aren't allowed and won't go through with it.

ℯ **1 mark for the first sentence. No marks for the second sentence because it is not specifically linked to statements within the program. 1 mark**

(c) IF (balance DIV 10 >= 0) AND (balance DIV 10 < 10) THEN

ℯ **No mark for balance DIV 10 >= 0 because it would allow 0. 1 mark for the AND. No mark for the final comparison. 1 mark**

Question 7 mark scheme

(a) 1 mark for each of the following points:
- DIV used to divide balance by 10.
- DIV removes the remainder, leaving the whole number part.
- Dividing by 10 ensures that the whole number part is a multiple of 10

(b) 1 mark for each of the following points:
- Negative values can still be divided by 10 and give negative answers.
- IF statement condition only checks for balance rounded to 0, not negative values.
- Negative values activate the ELSE clause, which displays the rounded negative value.

(c) 1 mark for each of the following points:
- balance DIV 10 > 0
- AND
- balance DIV 10 <= 10

Question 8
Student A

(a) Subroutines are blocks of code that are separate from the main program that are run by being called from the main program

ℯ **1 mark for identifying separate code, 1 mark for describing interaction with calling program. 2 marks**

(b)
```
username ← USERINPUT
part1 ← letters(username)
part2 ← numbers(username)
password = part1 + INT_TO_STRING(part2)
OUTPUT password
```

⊛ **1 mark for the letters subroutine called correctly, 1 mark for the numbers subroutine called correctly, 1 mark for string concatenation, 1 mark for of string conversion, 1 mark for password output. 5 marks**

(c) Modularised programs make programming the solution easier as smaller solutions can be coded and tested without affecting the main program. In the password program this means that the letter and number generation can be worked out separately and joined together later. Modular programs also make changes to the code easier. For example, if four letters were required from the first subroutine, the change could be located easily and changed in the subroutine rather than tracing through a large single block of code to find what needs to be changed.

⊛ **1 mark for the first sentence — it is easier to code and test smaller solutions. 1 mark for applying an advantage to the example. 1 mark — it is easier to make changes. 1 mark for applying an advantage to the example. 4 marks**

Question 8
Student B

(a) A subroutine is a smaller, separated block of code that doesn't interact with the main program.

⊛ **1 mark for identifying separate code, but no mark for the second point because subroutines are run from the main program and can pass data. 1 mark**

(b)
```
username ← USERINPUT
part1 ← letters(username)
part2 ← numbers(username)
password = part1 + part2
```

⊛ **1 mark for the letters subroutine called correctly, 1 mark for the numbers subroutine called correctly, 1 mark for string concatenation. The remaining 2 marks are not awarded because there is no string conversion and the password is not output. 3 marks**

(c) This modularised program has the advantage of being easy to read and follow. Anyone who wants to understand the working of the program will not have to read repeated blocks of code. It is also an advantage that the code is safer and cannot be changed in any way. This makes it easier to keep the password secret.

⊛ **1 mark for identifying an advantage in the first sentence. 1 mark for applying an advantage to the example. The second point is not an advantage, so no mark is awarded. 2 marks**

Question 8 mark scheme

(a) 1 mark for each of the following points:
- Separate block of code from main program.
- Called from main program when required to run.

(b) 1 mark for each of the following points:
- part1 ← letters(username)
- part2 ← numbers(username)
- password = part1 +…
- … INT_TO_STRING(part2)
- OUTPUT password

(c) 1 mark for each advantage (2 max.) and 1 mark for describing how it applies to the example (2 max.):
- It makes code easier to read…
- … complex password generation stages broken down into key components.
- It is easier to code and test the program…
- … stages of password generation can be coded and tested separately to ensure they work.
- Code reusability…
- … password generation functions can be repeated simply by calling the subroutine at other points in the program.

Question 9
Student A

(a) This array of scores can be given a common reference identifier whereby each score can be accessed by reference to an index value. This means the data can be easily accessed by the combination of the array name and index value.

e 1 mark for the use of an identifier, 1 mark for describing ease of access to data. **2 marks**

(b)
```
x ← 0
average ← 0
total ← 0
WHILE x < LEN(testScores)
    total ← total + testScores[x]
    x ← x + 1
ENDWHILE
average ← total / 5
```

e 1 mark for loop stops when x passes array end, 1 mark for total calculated in every iteration, 1 mark for loop counter incremented, 1 mark for average calculated after loop. **4 marks**

Question 9
Student B

(a) Arrays are useful for storing integers as they are collected together under one convenient name, which means the test data are easy to find

e 1 mark for identifying that the data are referenced by a single name, but the second mark is not awarded as the student doesn't explain why. **1 mark**

(b)
```
x ← 0
average ← 0
total ← 0
WHILE x <= LEN(testScores)
    total ← total + testScores[x]
ENDWHILE
average ← total / 5
```

e No mark for WHILE as it includes an extra pass through the loop, 1 mark for total calculated in every iteration, no mark as the loop counter is not incremented, 1 mark for average calculated after the loop. **2 marks**

Question 9 mark scheme

(a) 1 mark for each of the following points:
- An array will store test scores under one common name.
- The index value can be used to access any of the test scores by changing its value.

(b) 1 mark for each of the following points:
- Array condition stops after last array element.
- Total calculated within the loop.
- Loop counter incremented through the loop.
- Average calculated after loop finished.

Question 10
Student A

(a) High-level languages are structured in a similar way to natural human languages, compared to low-level which are often very short statements, which makes it easier for those creating programs to understand what has been written. Also it is quicker to write high-level code as simple functions produce many machine-code instructions which, if written in low-level, would take a long time to code.

e 1 mark for reference to high-level language being closer to written language than low-level language, which is closer to machine code. 1 mark for expanding on the benefit of ease of comprehension. 1 mark for identifying improved development time. 1 mark for explaining how high-level language speeds up development. **4 marks**

(b) A compiler takes an entire program as input and converts it into machine code as a whole before executing it. Interpreters are different because they complete the process a line at a time, running the program in the same way.

e 1 mark for identifying that compiled languages process the code all at once. 1 mark for contrasting this with interpretation, which achieves execution one line at a time. **2 marks**

Question 10
Student B

(a) High-level languages are easier for humans to read because the way they are written is closer to the way that humans speak compared to statements used in low-level. This makes high-level programs easier to read and understand. High-level is also quicker and fewer things go wrong.

e 1 mark for reference to high-level language being closer to written language than low-level language, which is closer to machine code. 1 mark for explaining the benefit. No marks for the last sentence as there is no context for the statements made. **2 marks**

(b) Compilers convert a whole program at once to machine code. Interpreters don't.

e 1 mark for identifying that compilers convert the whole program to machine code before the program is run. No mark for the second sentence because the interpretation process is not outlined. **1 mark**

Question 10 mark scheme

(a) 1 mark for each point (2 max.) and 1 mark for supporting explanation (2 max.):
- Closer to human language…
- …making it easier to read and understand.
- Shorter development time…
- …as statements and functions summarise machine-code sequences that would have to be coded directly in low-level.
- Language is portable…
- …can be compiled on different machine architectures.

(b) 1 mark for each of the following points:
- Compilers process the entire program at once to produce the equivalent machine code before running.
- Interpreters process code a line at a time and execute the translated machine code immediately.

1.3 Fundamentals of data representation

Question 11
Student A

(a) Decimal uses 10 symbols to count with, whereas binary uses only 2 (1 and 0). This means that counting continues in groups of 2 and each new place value represents a new group of 2.

e **This is a good explanation that covers both points. 2 marks**

(b)

Place value	128	64	32	16	8	4	2	1
Byte	1	1	1	1	1	0	1	0

e **All place values are correct (1), the conversion is correct (1). 2 marks**

(c) Hexadecimal values are determined using a range of 16 symbols. Base-16 is a multiple of base-2 and therefore these symbols match up with groups of four binary bits. Using the example, 1101 would be equivalent to D and 0011 to 3, giving the hex value D3. Hex provides a quick way of summarising binary values.

e **This student has identified that hex maps to binary values conveniently (1), shown how 4 bits map to a single hex value (1), given the correct conversion of the binary value (1) and explained that hex is used to summarise binary values in an easy-to-determine way (1). 4 marks**

Question 11
Student B

(a) Binary uses 1s and 0s to count values and make bigger numbers.

e **The student has identified that binary uses just two symbols (1), but has not given a description about counting in groups of 2, so the second mark is not awarded. 1 mark**

(b)

Place value	128	64	32	16	8	4	2	1
Byte	1	0	1	1	1	1	1	0

e **All place values are correct (1). The conversion has been done incorrectly, so no mark is awarded. 1 mark**

(c) Because hex has 16 values it relates to the same number of binary bits each time. So in the example, 11010011 becomes D3. This is so the computer can use D3 instead of 8 bits that don't make as much sense.

e **1 mark for identifying that hex maps to binary values conveniently, 1 mark for the correct conversion of the binary value. However, there is no explicit mention of how 4 bits map to a hex value (no marks). The student should have explained that data used in the computer are still binary but hex provides a more convenient summary for users (no marks). 2 marks**

Question 11 mark scheme

(a) 1 mark for each of the following points:
- Only two values/symbols are used in binary (1s and 0s).
- Counting is performed in groups of 2.

(b) 1 mark for each of the following points:
- All place values are correct — 64/32/16/8/4/2.
- The conversion is correct — 11111010.

(c) 1 mark for each of the following points (max. 4 marks):
- Hexadecimal values map directly to equivalent binary bits.
- Shows how four bits are equivalent to a single hexadecimal value.
- Correctly determines that 11010011 becomes D3.
- Hexadecimal values provide a convenient means to summarise binary data.
- Hexadecimal values are easier for humans to read and understand.
- Hexadecimal values are displayed more compactly.

Reject any answers that refer to saving storage space.

Question 12
Student A

(a) 10000010
     00000101
     00010100
     ─────────
     10011011
            1

e Each set of four bits is correct (2) and the carry is in the correct position (1). **3 marks**

(b) Bit shifting can be performed on binary values to move each original bit either to the left (010 becomes 100) or the right (010 becomes 001), creating a new value. Left shift is multiplying the value by 2 (doubling it) and right shift is dividing by 2 (halving it).

e This student has identified the left shift and explained with a correct example (1), identified the right shift and explained with a correct example (1), and stated that left shift is the equivalent of multiplying by 2 (1) and that right shift is the equivalent of dividing by 2 (1). **4 marks**

(c) Right bit shifting would allow the number of atoms to be halved each time. The input number of half-lives could then be used to right-shift the value an appropriate number of times. The resultant value would be the number of atoms left in the sample (in billions).

e This student has identified that right shifting could be used to halve the value (1), explained that the number of half-lives input could be used to determine how many shifts take place (1), and explained the result of shifting within the context of the question (1). **3 marks**

Question 12
Student B

(a) 10000010
    00000101
    00010100
    ─────────
    10010011

e Only the first four bits are correct (1); the third column from the right has not been calculated correctly. Carry has been missed in the third column: 1 + 1 + 0 = 10, therefore 1 is a carry, so no mark is awarded. **1 mark**

(b) You can have left shift (010 to 100) and right shift (010 to 1) to move the bits around in a binary value. Left shift increases the value by a factor of 2 (times 2) and right shift does the opposite.

e This student has identified left shift and explained with a correct example (1), and identified right shift, but the example should show that leading zeros are brought into the value (no marks). The student has identified that left shift multiplies by 2 (1), but needs to be more specific in what the opposite operation is (no marks). **2 marks**

(c) Left bit shifting is useful as you can tell how many atoms have decayed. The input number that represents the half-lives to work out could be useful as you could shift the value that amount of times.

e This student has mentioned but not correctly identified a type of shift and hasn't explained how bit shifting would be useful for working out the decay of the atoms (no marks). They have explained that the number of half-lives input could be used to determine how many shifts take place (1), but need to explain what the end result represents with regard to the example (no marks). **1 mark**

Question 12 mark scheme

(a) 1 mark for each of the following points:
- First four bits correct — 1001.
- Last four bits correct — 1011.
- Carry in third column from right.

(b) 1 mark for each of the following points:
- Left shift identified and explained with correct example: 010 becomes 100.
- Right shift identified and explained with correct example: 010 becomes 001.
- Identifies that left shift multiplies by 2 (double).
- Identifies that right shift divides by 2 (halve).

(c) 1 mark for each of the following points:
- Right shifting used to halve the value.
- Number of half-lives input used to determine how many shifts take place.
- Resulting values after shifts performed represent the halved value of atoms.

Question 13
Student A

(a) The analogue waves are sampled at regular intervals and the equivalent binary values are recorded and stored by the device.

e This student has identified that the wave is sampled/measured regularly (1) and has noted that samples are recorded as binary values (1). **2 marks**

(b) File size = rate × res × secs

10,000 × 8 × 20

= 1,600,000 bits

1,600,000/8

= 200,000 bytes

= 200 kB

e This student has outlined the calculation (1), has a correct initial answer (1), has divided by 8 to convert to bytes (1) and has provided the correct final answer (1). **4 marks**

(c) Pixels are single points of the image that are given a colour value based on the colour depth. The colour depth describes how many bits are used to describe each pixel, and different combinations of bits represent different colours.

e This student has explained that a pixel is a point on the image (1), has identified that each pixel is given a colour value (1) and has explained the relationship between colour depth, number of bits and number of colours (1). **3 marks**

(d) 600 × 300 × 4

= 720,000 bits

= 90,000 bytes

e Correct working out is shown (1) and the correct answer converted to bytes is given (1). **2 marks**

Question 13
Student B

(a) Analogue data are converted into binary numbers that represent the waves.

e This student has noted that binary values represent the measurements taken (1), but needs to be clear about the analogue wave being sampled at regular points in time (no marks). **1 mark**

(b) 10,000 × 8 × 20

= 1,600,000 bits

1,600,000/8

= 200,000 kB

(e) This student needs to identify which calculation to perform first (no marks), but has given a correct initial answer (1) and divided by 8 to convert to bytes (1). However, the student has not converted to kB, assuming that the answer is already in bytes (no marks). **2 marks**

(c) Pixels make up the image and each pixel is described by its colour, using a combination of bits (known as the colour depth). Colour depth expresses how many colours there are available.

(e) This student needs to be clear that a pixel is a point on a picture (no marks), but has related colour depth to the colour of each pixel (1). They need to explain that colour depth describes the number of bits used to describe the colour of each pixel (no marks). **1 mark**

(d) $600 \times 300 \times 4$
 $= 720,000$

(e) Correct working out is shown (1) but the answer has not been converted to bytes (no marks). **1 mark**

Question 13 mark scheme

(a) 1 mark for each of the following points:
- Analogue wave is sampled at regular intervals.
- Samples are stored as binary equivalent values.

(b) 1 mark for each of the following points:
- Explains that file size = sampling rate × resolution × seconds of audio.
- $10,000 \times 8 \times 20 = 1,600,000$ bits.
- $1,600,000/8 = 200,000$ bytes.
- 200 kB as final answer.

(c) 1 mark for each of the following points:
- Pixel is a point on an image.
- Each pixel is assigned a colour based on the colour depth.
- Colour depth determines how many bits are used to represent the colour of each pixel.

(d) 1 mark for each of the following points:
- Bit count of image calculated correctly as $600 \times 300 \times 4$.
- Answer expressed as bytes: 90,000 bytes.

Question 14
Student A

(a) The attachment may have been compressed in order to reduce the time taken to send. A smaller file attached to an email will take less time to send as there are fewer data to transfer. Also, the sender might be concerned about storage space in their mailbox. Smaller attachments will not use up their mailbox storage allocation as quickly as the uncompressed versions.

ⓔ This student has identified a reason for compressing the files (1), explained the benefit, in terms of send times, of compressing attachments (1), identified a second reason for compressing the files (1) and explained the benefit in terms of storage of the attachments in the mailbox (1). **4 marks**

(b) A — 00

D — 101

F — 111

ⓔ The correct answer is given for A, D and F. **3 marks**

(c) RLE summarises groups of characters so the number of occurrences replaces the actual characters. This means overall the file size is reduced as the numbers reduce the character count. In terms of the example, this would become 5A3B6A5D10F3E, saving 19 characters.

ⓔ This student has explained the RLE principle (1), explained how the coding reduces the size of the data (1) and illustrated the amount of compression using the example (1). **3 marks**

Question 14
Student B

(a) Compression of attachments lowers the time to send the email as it makes things faster. Also, they might be concerned about the bandwidth usage on their broadband.

ⓔ This student has identified a reason for compressing the files (1), but needs to explain why it is faster (no marks). The student has identified a second reason for compressing the files (1), but needs to explain how reducing the attachment file size reduces the bandwidth requirements (no marks). **2 marks**

(b) A — 000

D — 101

F — 111

ⓔ An extra zero is included at front of A (no marks), the correct answer is given for D (1) and for F (1). **2 marks**

(c) RLE takes out bits of a message you don't need so it makes it smaller. Characters are reduced as sequences of the same characters are summarised using numbers. So for example AAAA would become 4A.

> **This student has not explained the principle of RLE (no marks), but has explained how RLE is able to achieve compression (1). The student has not used the example provided (no marks). 1 mark**

Question 14 mark scheme

(a) 1 mark for each of the following points and 1 mark for the associated explanation (max. two points with explanations per student response):
- Reduce send time…
- …compressed files have fewer data and therefore do not take as long to transfer, thus reducing the wait time.
- Reduce bandwidth usage…
- …reduced data transfer requirement uses up less bandwidth as part of the transfer.
- Reduce storage of attachments…
- …email mailboxes have to store the attachments, therefore a compressed file will reduce the space requirements.

(b) 1 mark for each of the following points:
- A — 00
- D — 101
- F — 111

(c) 1 mark for each of the following points:
- Describes the general principle of RLE (patterns of the same character summarised with a numerical value).
- Describes how RLE compresses data (fewer characters used to store the number rather than all the characters themselves).
- Explains how the example would be reduced (it becomes 5A3B6A5D10F3E).

1.4 Computer systems

Question 15
Student A

(a) Logic gates are building blocks of more complicated circuits. They build the hardware components that computer systems control to carry out instructions provided by the software.

e This student has explained that logic gates are combined into more complex hardware (1) and that these hardware components are controlled by software (1). **2 marks**

(b)

A	B	C	Q
0	0	0	1
0	0	1	0
0	1	0	1
0	1	1	0
1	0	0	1
1	0	1	0
1	1	0	0
1	1	1	0

e 1 mark is awarded for each of the last four rows completed correctly. **4 marks**

(c)
- I/O devices — when signalled, switches from task performing to move data in or out of the computer.
- Security — controls who can access the system and its data.
- Processor — controls which parts of a program need to run and switches between all competing requirements.

e This student has explained that the OS controls movement of data in or out of the computer (1), identified that the OS controls access to the system and resources (1) and identified control management of differing program threads (1). **3 marks**

Question 15
Student B

(a) Logic gates are combined to make circuits that form hardware components. These control the computer system to do actions.

e This student has explained that logic gates are combined into more complex hardware (1), but doesn't explain how software controls the hardware to perform required actions (no marks). **1 mark**

(b)

A	B	C	Q
0	0	0	1
0	0	1	0
0	1	0	1
0	1	1	0
1	0	0	0
1	0	1	0
1	1	0	0
1	1	1	1

(e) For the first row completed, no mark is awarded — output from OR gate will be 0 which is inverted at the end. 1 mark for the next row, which is completed correctly. 1 mark for the third row completed correctly. No mark is given for the last row — output from OR gate will be 1 which is inverted at the end. **2 marks**

(c)
- I/O devices — controls how data move in and out of computer through I/O device.
- Security — checks to see if a user is allowed on to the system or has permission to access stored data.
- Processor — instructs.

(e) This student has explained that the OS controls movement of data in or out of the computer (1) and has identified that the OS controls access to the system and resources (1). The processor is designed to carry out operations on data and the OS does not do this, so no mark is awarded. **2 marks**

Question 15 mark scheme

(a) 1 mark for each of the following points:
- Logic gates are combined to make more complex circuits (the hardware of the computer system).
- These circuits are controlled by software to produce desired outputs.

(b) 1 mark for each correct outcome: 1, 0, 0, 0 (in order).

(c) 1 mark for each of the following points:
- I/O devices — interfaces with input and output hardware to control the flow of data in and out of the computer system.
- Security — checks if a user can gain entry to the computer system and has appropriate permissions to access its data.
- Processor — OS switches between currently running programs.

Question 16
Student A

(a) There is only one area of memory in a Von Neumann machine. The memory stores both the instructions and the data together. Memory access is entirely random and the data and instructions can be stored and retrieved from any location.

e This student has identified that there is only one area for memory (1) and has explained that data and instructions are stored together in this single location (1) and that memory access is random and that data and instructions have no limitation on where they can be located (1). **3 marks**

(b) The ALU is responsible for carrying out any arithmetic and logic functions to produce a useable output. Instructions from programs stored in memory are executed and used to control the functions the ALU should perform.

e This student has noted that outputs are produced for arithmetic and logical operations (1) and that instructions from programs are used to control the operation of the ALU (1). **2 marks**

(c) The first part of the cycle is known as the fetch. This is where the instruction to be executed is retrieved from memory ready to be worked on. Next, the decode part of the cycle is executed. The instruction that was fetched is decoded by the control unit so that the operation to perform can be identified. Lastly, the execute stage carries out the instruction decoded by enabling other parts of the computer as necessary.

e This student has explained that the fetch part of the cycle brings the next instruction to be executed into the processor (1), that the decode cycle determines what action should be performed by the instruction (1) and that the decoded instruction is then carried out by the processor (1). **3 marks**

Question 16
Student B

(a) In Von Neumann architecture the machine knows where the data and instructions should be kept. This can be in the same memory area and stored together because it is segmented into a part only for instructions and a part for data.

e This student has not been specific in explaining how many memory locations there are (no marks), but has explained that data and instructions are stored together (1). The student has not explained that memory access is random and that data and instructions can be stored in any location (no marks). **1 mark**

(b) The ALU works things out based on instructions processed. The instructions from programs being executed let the ALU know what to do.

e This student has not specifically mentioned outputs produced from arithmetic and/or logic operations (no marks), but has noted that instructions from programs are used to control the operation of the ALU (1). **1 mark**

(c) The first part of this cycle is called the fetch. This is where everything needed by the processor is retrieved from memory. Then an instruction is decoded so that what to do with it can be determined so that the processor can inform the appropriate part for the execute stage, which is last.

This student has not specifically mentioned that instructions are retrieved from memory (no marks), but has identified that the instruction is decoded (1). The third mark is not awarded because the student hasn't explained the purpose of the execute stage. 1 mark

Question 16 mark scheme

(a) 1 mark for each of the following points:
- Only one main area for memory.
- Data and instructions stored together.
- Memory access is random and data/instructions can be stored in any location.

(b) 1 mark for each of the following points:
- Completes arithmetic operations like addition and subtraction.
- Completes logical operations such as the comparsion of two numbers.
- Instructions from programs are used to signal the ALU to carry out an appropriate action on its inputs.

(c) 1 mark for each of the following clear descriptions of the stage:
- Fetch — retrieves next instruction to work on from memory.
- Decode — decodes the instruction retrieved previously to control the processor appropriately to carry out this instruction.
- Execute — instruction previously decoded is carried out to produce a required output.

Question 17
Student A

(a) Non-volatile storage is where data are stored and are retained when the power to the storage device is turned off. This is different from volatile storage, such as main memory, where if the power is turned off, the data are lost.

e This student has defined the meaning of non-volatile (1), given a suitable example of volatile storage (1) and contrasted the effect of power loss on volatile storage compared to non-volatile (1). **3 marks**

(b) Solid state: electrical circuits are used to persistently store data until they are changed, even when the power is off. Optical: data are etched onto a reflective surface that can be read when an optical light source is shined off it.

e Solid state: This student has identified the name of secondary storage (1) and explained that electrical circuits store the data (1).
Optical: They have identified the name of secondary storage (1) and explained that data stored on a reflective surface can be read again by the reflections of an optical light source (1). **4 marks**

(c) Cloud storage is where data are not stored locally but in a place where you can gain access to them from the internet. One benefit of using it is that the files are accessible anywhere where you have a connection to the internet. This is better than local storage as the files are only usually available at that local machine.

e This student has explained that cloud storage is physically separate from the computer being used (1), has identified an advantage of cloud storage (1) and has explained the benefit (1). **3 marks**

Question 17
Student B

(a) Non-volatile means that data aren't lost. Volatile memory does lose data, for example RAM memory storage.

e This student needs to be clear that the removal of power to the device doesn't result in data loss (no marks), and must clearly identify the need for power to sustain the data (no marks). A suitable example is identified (1). **1 mark**

(b) Solid state: this is where memory never loses its data.

DVD: reflective disc contains data that are read by a laser shined back off it.

e Solid state: This student has identified the name of secondary storage (1) but hasn't explained why this is the case (no marks).
DVD: They need to specify the generic form of storage rather than a specific implementation (no marks), but they have identified that a reflective surface stores data that are read by an optical source (1). **2 marks**

(c) Cloud storage is where data are stored in the cloud. One benefit is that the data are backed up somewhere safe.

ⓔ This student needs to explain what the cloud refers to and how it is different from other storage methods (no marks), but has identified a benefit (1). They must explain how cloud storage is 'safer' for backups than alternative storage means (no marks). **2 marks**

Question 17 mark scheme

(a) 1 mark for each of the following points:
- Non-volatile — data remain even if the power source is turned off.
- Volatile — data are lost when power is turned off.
- Suitable example of volatile storage — e.g. main memory.

(b) 1 mark for each of the following points:
- Solid state…
- …electrical circuits store data until written over, even when the power is removed.
- Optical…
- …reflective disc contains data that are read by a light source that measures the reflections to re-create the data.

(c) 1 mark for the definition: Cloud storage is storage that is not physically located with the host computer but is accessible using internet services.

1 mark for identifying an advantage (1 max.) and describing why it is better than local storage (1 max.):
- Access to data anywhere there is an internet connection…
- …local storage is limited to the physical place where you gain access to the computer.
- Backups of data can be kept safely…
- …cloud storage is physically separate from the host computer, therefore it is not susceptible to the same physical threats.
- Can be easily expanded…
- …physical storage is difficult to expand as it consists of physical devices, whereas cloud storage can be added to easily.
- Enables collaboration…
- …multiple users can share the same documents at the same time without providing any specialist software.

Question 18
Student A

(a) Cache memory is high speed and is located very close to the processor itself. A larger cache means that more data can be stored for immediate access by the processor, rather than having to be retrieved from main memory which is slower. There are different types of cache known as different levels. Each level of cache performs faster and can retrieve data much more quickly. Cache improves performance by reducing the time it takes for data to be retrieved and processed.

(e) **This student has explained that a larger cache stores more data that can be retrieved more quickly (1), has distinguished between different levels of cache and their reduced time to provide the data for the processor (1) and has recognised that cache reduces the processor waiting time to retrieve data (1). 3 marks**

(b) The clock speed refers to the number of cycles the processor can perform per second. The higher the frequency of the clock, the more cycles there will be and therefore the faster the processor will get things done. Also, processors can be made with more than one core. This means there are multiple processors operating in the computer working in parallel. As the processor can work on multiple tasks it doesn't have to wait for other jobs to complete, therefore getting more things done in a shorter time.

(e) **This student has identified what clock speed is (1), explained why a higher clock speed improves performance (1), described what the number of cores means (1) and explained the benefit of parallel execution (1). 4 marks**

(c) System software is used for the operation and maintenance of a computer system, whereas application software is for a user to carry out tasks on the system. System software can be used to improve the performance of hardware in the system. For example, a disk defragmenter can be used to bring together parts of a file stored on a hard disk in order to improve the access time of files.

(e) **The difference between system and application software has been explained (1), an example identified (1) and how the software improves performance of the system is explained (1). 3 marks**

Question 18
Student B

(a) Cache is useful because it reduces the time the processor waits in order to retrieve data it needs to use. The bigger the cache and the better the type, the faster the processor will run because it is better than normal RAM.

(e) **This student has recognised that cache reduces the processor waiting time to retrieve data (1), but needs to explain that cache has faster access time and, if larger, can store more frequently used data (no marks). 1 mark**

(b) A faster clock speed means that there are more pulses in a second that controls the processor, meaning that it gets more things done in a shorter time. Having more cores also improves things as there are effectively more processors available to the computer system to do work.

⊚ **This student needs to be more specific in explaining what a clock does (no marks), but has explained why a higher clock speed improves performance (1) and has identified what more cores mean (1). The student needs to explain why more cores benefit the performance of the system (no marks). 2 marks**

(c) System software lets the user do things on a computer and applications software allows the user to do things they could also do without a computer. For example, a start-up manager allows the user to select what programs to load when the computer starts.

⊚ **The definition could also include application software, so it needs to be clearer (no marks). The student has identified an example of system software (1), but needs to explain how the software improves system performance (no marks). 1 mark**

Question 18 mark scheme

(a) 1 mark for each of the following points:
- Reduces time to retrieve data as it is comparatively faster than main memory.
- Larger cache can store more frequently used data so that the processor can access it more often.
- Cache types improve performance at each level using faster access time.

(b) 1 mark for each of the following points:
- Clock speed defined as number of cycles per second on which the processor can be triggered to carry out an action.
- Increased clock speed reduces the time between triggers, resulting in more operations carried out in the same period of time.
- Number of cores is the number of processor units that can carry out instructions.
- More cores can execute more instructions in parallel, reducing the wait time between completion of instructions.

(c) 1 mark for each of the following points:
- System software is used to maintain and operate a computer system.
- Valid example (defrag utility/memory manager/start-up tuner/file duplication remover/registry optimiser/or any other valid software).
- Explanation of how software improves performance (moves file fragments together/reduces unused programs loaded to memory/removes unneeded registry entries to improve load times/etc.).

Paper 2 Written assessment

2.1 Fundamentals of data representation

Example responses

> **Question 1**
> Student A
>
> (a) 2   ○
>   10   ○
>   16   ●
>
> ⓔ This student has correctly identified 16. **1 mark**
>
> (b) 154
>
> ⓔ This is the correct answer. **1 mark**
>
> (c) 01100000
>
> ⓔ This is correctly converted from decimal number to binary. **1 mark**
>
> (d) 242
>
> ⓔ The hexadecimal number has been converted correctly to decimal. **1 mark**
>
> (e) The smallest number is 0, the largest is 11111111 = 255.
>
> ⓔ The smallest number (1) and the largest (1) are correct. **2 marks**
>
> (f) 3 GB   ○
>   2000 kB   ○
>   3001 MB   ●
>
> ⓔ This student has correctly identified 3001 MB. **1 mark**

> **Question 1**
> Student B
>
> (a) 2   ○
>   10   ●
>   16   ●
>
> ⓔ This student has shaded two lozenges. Even though the correct answer has been shaded, this is cancelled out by the incorrect one. No mark is awarded.
>
> (b) 152
>
> ⓔ This is an incorrect answer. Answers should always be double-checked, as this is very close. No mark is awarded.

(c) 1100000

ⓔ This student has correctly converted the decimal number to binary, but the question asked for the answer in 8 bits. This answer has only 7 bits, so no mark is awarded

(d) 18

ⓔ This conversion is incorrect, so no mark is awarded.

(e) The smallest number is 1, the largest is 255.

ⓔ This student has correctly identified the largest as 255 (1), but the smallest is incorrect as 0 can also be stored by having all the bits as 0. **1 mark**

(f) 3 GB ●
2000 kB ○
3001 MB ○

ⓔ This student has given the incorrect answer. 3 GB is equivalent to 3000 MB, therefore 3001 MB is larger. No mark is awarded.

Question 1 mark scheme

(a) 1 mark for the correct answer. No marks if more than one lozenge is shaded.
- 2   ○
- 10 ○
- 16 ●

(b) 1 mark for the correct answer: 154.

(c) 1 mark for the correct answer: 01100000.

(d) 1 mark for the correct answer: 242. Working (not required for answer): (F * 16) + 2 = (15 * 16) + 2 = 240 + 2.

(e) 1 mark for the smallest, 1 mark for the largest.
- Smallest = 0
- Largest = 255

(f) 1 mark for the correct answer. No marks if more than one lozenge is shaded.
- 3 GB   ○
- 2000 kB   ○
- 3001 MB   ●

Question 2
Student A

(a) An image from a photograph is a bitmap. A bitmap is made up of coloured squares called pixels. The colours in the pixels all have their own binary number, the binary is put together, one after the other to say what colour every pixel is.

ⓔ **This student has correctly identified that the image is made up of pixels (1), that each colour has its own unique binary number (1) and that these binary numbers are stored in the file (1). 3 marks**

(b) The colour image can have 2^24 different colours, because each colour will have its own unique 24-bit code. This is a good colour depth because there are more shades so the image looks more realistic.

ⓔ **This student has correctly stated that there are 2^24 different colours available (1) and that each colour has 24 bits (1). 2 marks**

(c) The image now has fewer bits per pixel; this means there are fewer colours, so fewer shades. The image won't be as clear, or as close to the original, because it has fewer colours. The file will be smaller in size because there is the same number of pixels, but fewer bits per pixel, so fewer bits to store overall.

ⓔ **This student has correctly identified that the image quality will decrease (1), explained why this is (1), correctly stated that the file size will decrease as well (1) and explained why this will happen (1). 4 marks**

(d)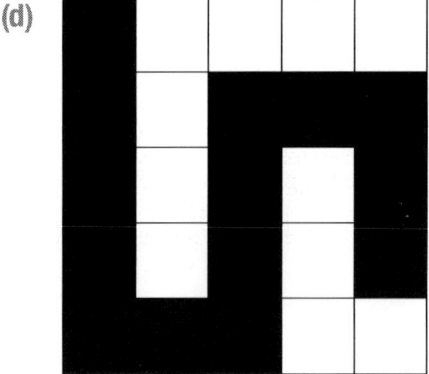

ⓔ **This student has correctly reproduced the image as a 5 by 5 image. 5 marks**

Question 2
Student B

(a) The photograph is taken and stored in binary by the camera. The camera captures the different colours and each one has a binary number. The binary numbers for the colours are stored to make the picture.

ⓔ **This student has correctly identified that each colour has its own binary number (1), and that the binary for the colours is stored — this could have been improved by referring to the pixels, but a mark can be awarded for this (1). 2 marks**

(b) This means that there are 24 bits of 1 and 0 for every colour, so every pixel has 24 bits.

ⓔ **This student has correctly identified that each colour has 24 bits (1). 1 mark**

(c) Fewer bits = fewer bits per pixel = fewer bits overall = smaller file size.

(e) **This student has correctly identified that the file size will decrease (1) and stated that this is because there are fewer bits per pixel (1). The question asked for two effects and this student has given only one, so can access only two of the marks. 2 marks**

(d)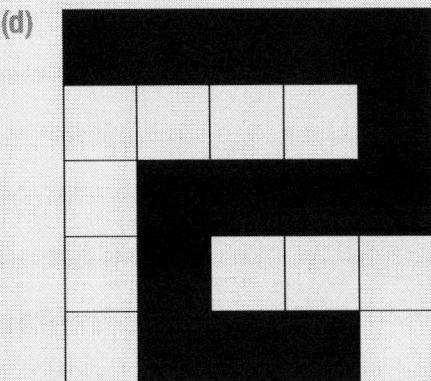

(e) **This student has correctly followed the binary, but has moved down rather than across, which means the image is incorrect. No mark is awarded.**

Question 2 mark scheme

(a) 3 marks from:
- The photograph is a series of pixels.
- Each pixel has a single colour.
- Each colour has a unique binary number.
- The binary numbers for the pixels are stored in order in the file.

(b) 1 mark for each of the following points:
- Each colour has a unique 24-bit colour.
- This means there are 2^24 different colours.
- This colour of each pixel is represented by a 24 bit number.

(c) 1 mark for each of the following points:
- The file size will decrease…
- …because there are fewer bits per pixel.
- The quality of the image will decrease…
- …because there are fewer colours that can be used

(d) 1 mark for each correct row

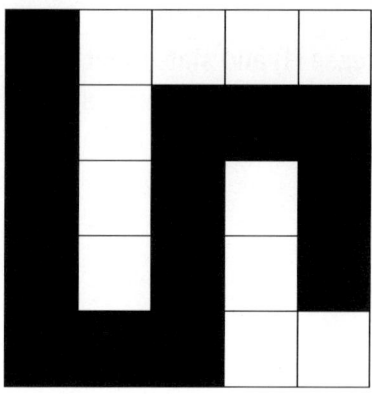

Question 3
Student A

(a) 0 0 1 0 1 1 1 0
    1 0 1 1 1 1 0 1
    ―――――――
    1 1 1 0 1 0 1 1
      1 1 1 1

e This student has correctly added together the two binary numbers (1) and shown where bits have been carried in the process (1). **2 marks**

(b) 0 0 0 0 0 1 1 0
    1 0 1 0 1 1 0 1
    0 0 1 0 0 1 1 0
    ―――――――
    1 1 0 1 1 0 0 1
      1 1 1

e This student has correctly added together the three binary numbers, both nibbles are correct (2) and the student has shown the working in the carry bits (1). **3 marks**

(c) 00011001

e The binary number is correctly shifted two places to the right. **1 mark**

(d) 01101011000

e The binary number is correctly shifted three places to the left. **1 mark**

(e) The binary number will be multiplied by 4.

e A left shift involves multiplication (1) and a 2-place shift is multiplying by 4 (1). **2 marks**

(f) The binary number will be divided by 8.

e A right shift involves division (1) and a three-place shift involves dividing by 8 (1). **2 marks**

Question 3
Student B

(a) 00101110
    10111101
    ─────────
    01101011

- This student has not shown the carry bits, which constitute the working. The MSB (most significant bit) is also incorrect. It is important that carry bits are shown, as this helps with knowing how many bits need adding. **No mark is awarded.**

(b) 00000110
    10101101
    00100110
    ─────────
    11001001
      1   1

- This student got the correct result for the right nibble (1) but incorrectly added together the four 1s; these should result in 0 and carry over left two bit positions. This also means that the working is incorrect. **1 mark**

(c) 0001100100

- This student has added additional 0s to the front of the binary number, but needed to remove the same number of 0s from the right-hand side of the number. **No mark is awarded.**

(d) 00001101011

- This student has not performed a shift on the number and the binary digits should have moved to the left, with the additional 0s placed on the right-hand side. **No marks are awarded.**

(e) A left shift multiplies by 2.

- This student has correctly stated that a left shift performs multiplication (1). Each shift does multiply by 2, so a 2-place shift multiplies by 4. Students should make sure that they are applying their knowledge to the scenario in the question. **1 mark**

(f) A right shift divides by 6.

- This student has correctly stated that a right shift performs division (1). Each shift increases the division by a power of 2, so a 2-place shift is 2^2 = 4, a 3-place is 2^2^2 = 8. **1 mark**

Question 3 mark scheme

(a) 1 mark for the answer, 1 mark for the carry bits:

    00101110
    10111101
    ─────────
    11101011
      1111

(b) 1 mark for each nibble, 1 mark for the working (carries):

```
  0 0 0 0 0 1 1 0
  1 0 1 0 1 1 0 1
  0 0 1 0 0 1 1 0
  _____
  1 1 0 1 1 0 0 1
      1   1   1
```

(c) 1 mark for the correct answer: 00011001.

(d) 1 mark for the correct answer: 01101011000.

(e) 1 mark for each of the following points:
  ▷ Multiplies the number…
  ▷ …by 4.

(f) 1 mark for each of the following points:
  ▷ Divides the number …
  ▷ … by 8.

Question 4
Student A

(a) A character set like ASCII has all of the letters and numbers and symbols such as # and @ which that particular computer can have entered and can store.

e **The character set is correctly described as all the symbols (1) that the computer can store (1). 2 marks**

(b) Unicode has more bits per character, it can have up to 2 bytes, but ASCII is only max. 1 byte per character. The fewer bits mean the fewer characters it can store.

e **This student has correctly identified that Unicode is 32 bits (1) and that ASCII is 8 bits (1). They have also described how ASCII stores fewer bits, but the maximum marks for this question have already been attained. 2 marks**

(c) One benefit of using Unicode is that it has more bits per character. This means that it can store more characters, e.g. those from other languages. One drawback is that because there are more characters, there are more bits per character so the file becomes larger.

e **This student has identified that Unicode can store more characters (1), given a suitable example (1) and explained that there are more bits per character (1), which means that the file size is larger (1). 4 marks**

(d) 01001010

e **This is the correct answer. 1 mark**

(e) If you enter a postcode in lowercase, and it is stored in uppercase, then it may not be recognised. A lowercase letter, e.g. a, has a different character code to the same letter in uppercase, e.g. A. The character codes from the character set are compared and because they are different, a and A are not the same.

e This student has correctly identified that the letters are saved using the character set (1), that uppercase and lowercase characters have different codes (1) and has said that the character codes for the two letters are compared (1). **3 marks**

Question 4
Student B

(a) Unicode is a character set, it's letters and numbers.

e This student has given an example of a character set, which was not asked for in the question. The student has also said that it is the letters and numbers, but a character set may be more than just these, e.g. symbols, and this is not clear in the answer. No mark is awarded.

(b) ASCII and Unicode can store different characters. Unicode can store all characters for all languages, but ASCII can't store that many.

e This student has correctly identified that Unicode can store more characters (1). To get an additional mark, the student would need to expand this to say why. **1 mark**

(c) One benefit is there is a better range of letters and numbers, like á which ASCII cannot always show. One drawback is that it is more complicated because there are more letters and numbers.

e This student has correctly identified that Unicode can store more (1), although it does not only store letters and numbers, and also given an example (1). The drawback needs to have more detail about what is complicated, so this does not get any marks. **2 marks**

(d) 01000110

e This answer is incorrect. If E is the binary number 69, then F is 70, G is 71, H is 72, I is 73, so J is 74. No mark is awarded.

(e) S1 4UY is not the same as s1 4uy because S might be stored with 01010101 and s is 101010101. These are not the same.

e This student has identified that the letters are saved as binary numbers in the examples given (1) and demonstrated an understanding that lowercase and uppercase letters have different codes (1). **2 marks**

Question 4 mark scheme

(a) 1 mark for each of the following points (max. 2 marks):
- A defined list of characters/symbols…
- … that can be recognised by a computer/stored by a computer.
- Represented by a binary/numerical value.

(b) 2 marks from:
- ASCII is 7/8 bits.
- Unicode is 16/32 bits.
- Unicode can store more characters than ASCII.

(c) 1 mark for each of the following points:

Benefits:
- Unicode allows a greater range of characters.
- It can store characters from other languages as well.

Drawbacks:
- File size will be larger.
- There are more bits per character.

(d) The correct answer is 01001010.

(e) 3 marks from:
- Each letter is saved as a binary number…
- …using a character set.
- The binary numbers/character codes of the characters are compared.
- Lowercase and uppercase letters have different binary numbers.

Question 5
Student A

(a) The analogue sound is a sound wave. The height of the wave is measured thousands of times a second, with the same time between each sample; this is the sample rate. The height is stored as a binary number and all the numbers are stored together to make the file.

e **This student has identified that the frequency (wave height) is measured (1), at set intervals (1), and that these are stored as binary numbers (1). 3 marks**

(b) Each sample is stored as a series of bits and the number of bits used for each sample is the sample resolution, e.g. 8 bits per sample.

e **Sample resolution is correctly defined as the number of bits per sample (1). 1 mark**

(c) The sample rate is the number of samples taken per second and is measured in Hz.

e **This is the correct definition of sample rate (1). 1 mark**

(d) Sample rate × resolution × seconds.

e **This is the correct formula. 2 marks**

(e) Image size = 1000 × 500 = 500,000

No. bytes = 500,000 × 8 = 4,000,000

No. kB = 4,000,000/1000 = 4000

No. MB = 4000/1000 = 4

e The image size is calculated correctly (1), then multiplied by the colour depth (1) and then divided correctly to find the number of MB (2). **4 marks**

(f) Compression reduces the file size of a file.

e This is the purpose of compression. **1 mark**

(g) Instead of storing the binary numbers for every single pixel, you store the number of 0s and number of 1s repeatedly and then this is turned back into the binary. For example, if the image is stored as 10000011111100101, this could be 115061201110111.

e This student has correctly identified that the numbers of 0s (1) and 1s are stored (1) and has shown this applied in a suitable example (1). **3 marks**

Question 5
Student B

(a) Samples are taken of the sound wave every second and these are stored as binary numbers.

e This student has identified that samples are taken, but hasn't explained what is being sampled. The response also says that they are taken every second, but they are taken many times a second. The student has correctly identified that the samples are stored in binary (1). **1 mark**

(b) The sample resolution is the total number of bits.

e This is incorrect, because the total number of bits will be those used from every sample. No mark is awarded.

(c) The sample rate is how many times the height of the wave is measured.

e This is almost correct. This student has identified that it is the number of times it is measured, but needs to be clear that this is over a set period of time, i.e. a second. No mark is awarded.

(d) File size of one sample × number of samples.

e This student has given one correct multiplication (1), but this is not precise enough to gain both marks. The student may not know how many samples there are, so this needed to be expanded. **1 mark**

(e) 1000 × 500 × 8 = 4,000,000

e This student has correctly multiplied together the image dimensions (1) and the colour depth (1), but they have not converted the answer into MB. **2 marks**

(f) Compression is needed to so that files can fit on the computer.

e This may be a use of compression, but the purpose is what it actually does to the file, which is to reduce the file size. No mark is awarded.

(g) The colours are stored and also how many pixels have that colour.

e This student has correctly identified that the colour is stored (1), along with the number of pixels in that colour (1). The question asked for an example, which the student did not give.

2 marks

Question 5 mark scheme

(a) 1 mark for each of the following points:
- Frequency of wave is measured…
- …at set intervals/time intervals, e.g. every 1/1000th of a second.
- Frequency is recorded as a binary number.

(b) 1 mark for the number of bits stored/allocated per sample.

(c) 1 mark for the number of samples taken per second.

(d) 1 mark for correctly giving one multiplication, 1 mark for the complete formula. Allow any appropriate interpretation.

Sample rate × resolution × number of seconds

(e) 1 mark for each of the following points:
- 1000 × 500 = 500,000
- 500,000 × 8 = 4,000,000 Bytes
- 400,000/1000 = 4000 kB
- 4000/100 = 4 MB

(f) 1 mark for: to reduce the file size.

(g) 2 marks for the description, 1 mark for an example related to an image:
- Store the colour of a pixel…
- …and the number of times that colour pixel appears side by side…
- …e.g. R 3 B 4.

or
- Store the number of 0s and 0 (accept in example)…
- …and the number of 1s and 1 (accept in example)…
- …e.g. 6 0 2 1 3 0.

2.2 Computer systems

Question 6
Student A

(a) [diagram: A into AND gate; B and C into OR gate, output through NOT gate, into AND gate]

(e) All three gates have been added correctly. **3 marks**

(b)

A	B	C	NOT (B OR C)	Output
0	0	0	1	0
0	0	1	1	1
0	1	0	0	0
0	1	1	0	0
1	0	0	0	0
1	0	1	0	0
1	1	0	0	0
1	1	1	0	0

(e) This student has correctly worked through the logic circuit and all the outputs are correct.

4 marks

(c) ((NOT A) AND B) OR (NOT C)

(e) This student has correctly stated the logic circuit and used brackets to clearly show the order of precedence, although these are not all necessary. **3 marks**

Question 6
Student B

(a)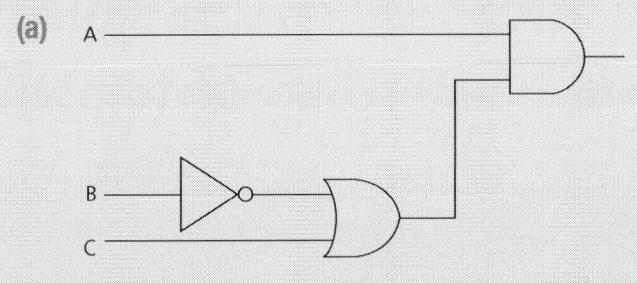

e This student has mixed the NOT and OR gates, as the NOT is applied to the whole of B OR C. The AND gate is in the correct place (even though NOT (B OR C) is incorrect), so 1 mark is awarded. **1 mark**

(b)

A	B	C	NOT (B OR C)	Output
0	0	0	0	0
0	0	1	0	0
0	1	0	0	0
0	1	1	0	0
1	0	0	0	0
1	0	1	0	0
1	1	0	0	0
1	1	1	0	0

e In the first two rows, this student has put that 0 OR 0 = 1. This is incorrect, so the first two row outputs are incorrect, losing 1 mark. The other answers are correct. **3 marks**

(c) NOT(NOT A AND B OR C)

e This student has correctly given NOT A AND B (1) and the OR is in the correct place (1). The NOT in the diagram only applies to C; in the answer it applies to everything, so is incorrect.

2 marks

Question 6 mark scheme

(a) 1 mark for each correct gate.

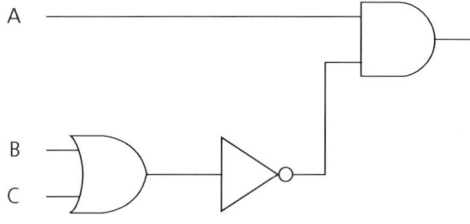

(b) 1 mark for each pair of rows completed correctly.

A	B	C	NOT (B OR C)	Output
0	0	0	1	0
0	0	1	1	1
0	1	0	0	0
0	1	1	0	0
1	0	0	0	0
1	0	1	0	0
1	1	0	0	0
1	1	1	0	0

(c) The correct answer is NOT A AND B OR NOT C. 1 mark for each of the following points, all required in the correct place:
- NOT A AND B
- NOT C
- OR

Question 7
Student A

(a) System software is what lets the application software talk to the hardware. Application software is what people use on the computer to do things, like listen to music, browse the internet and write word-processed documents.

ⓔ This student has correctly identified that system software lets the application software run (1) and that application software is for the user to perform tasks (1). 2 marks

(b) System software: the operating system and utility programs.

Application software: word processor, internet browser.

ⓔ The two examples of system software (2) and two examples of application software (2) are correct. 4 marks

(c) The PC could be upgraded by increasing the amount of RAM it has. RAM stores all currently running programs and data, so the more RAM you have, the more data and programs you can have running. If your PC is running short on RAM, then it uses virtual memory, which is slower to access than RAM, so by having enough RAM, the VM is not used as much.

Secondly, you could get a new motherboard with a faster CPU; the CPU will have a faster clock speed, e.g. 3.8 GHz instead of 2.5 GHz. More GHz means more processes that can run per second. You could even get a dual core or quad core if you don't already have one. This means that programs designed to run on multi-core processors can split the tasks between the cores and run faster.

(e) This student has identified that the RAM can be increased (1) and has given two explanations of how this improves the performance (2). They have identified that a new CPU could be purchased (1) and have given two explanations of how this improves the performance (2). **6 marks**

Question 7
Student B

(a) System software lets the computer run, application software is databases and other software that people use.

(e) This student has identified that application software is used by people (1), but the definition of system software is not quite detailed enough to gain the mark. **1 mark**

(b) System software is software to run the hardware like device drivers. Application software lets the user do things, like write letters in Microsoft Word.

(e) This student has correctly identified one example of system software; a driver is an example of a utility program (1). They have described the use of one application software and then given a brand name for the type, which is not awarded the mark. You need to make sure you are referring to generic types of software, which in this case would be a word processor.
1 mark

(c) You could get a better CPU so it can run tasks faster. This is good as you can play better games. You could also overclock the current CPU, which means that it can run faster, but you have to be careful to not overclock too much or it will overheat.

(e) This student has identified that a better CPU could be purchased (1), but has not explained how this allows tasks to be run faster. They have also identified that you could overclock the PC (1) but, again, they need to be more technical about why and how the computer is improved. **2 marks**

Question 7 mark scheme

(a) 1 mark for each of the following points:
- System software controls the hardware/acts as an interface between the applications and hardware.
- Application software is programs that the end users use/perform tasks for the user.

(b) Max. 2 marks for system software, max. 2 marks for application software. The answers given here are examples only.

System software:
- OS/operating system
- utility program/examples, e.g. device driver, defragmentation

Application software:
- word processor
- database
- spreadsheet

(c) Max. 3 marks for each method of upgrade (max. two upgrades), 1 mark for naming, max. 2 marks for explanation. The upgrades given here are examples; others are also valid:
- add more RAM
- increase the number of processes/applications running simultaneously
- decrease use of VM

- new CPU (and motherboard)
- faster processor = more processes carried out per second
- additional cores = more processes carried out at the same time

- overclock
- processes carried out at each clock cycle
- more cycles per second = more processes per second

Question 8
Student A

(a) One utility program is system clean-up. This scans all the files on the computer and removes any temp files like those downloaded from the internet to save space.

A second utility program is anti-virus software. This checks any files that you download and if there is a virus it deletes it. You can also scan your computer and if it finds any viruses it deletes them.

This student has correctly identified system clean-up (1) and described its purpose (1). The student has given a second utility as anti-virus (1) and described this (1). 4 marks

(b) The OS is vital to allow the user to interact with the hardware. It provides an interface, e.g. Windows is a GUI, so that the user can type in commands, click on buttons and the OS does what the user wants.

The OS manages many things in the computer; it manages the hardware, the memory, the software. The OS gets data from the RAM and sends them to the hard drive, or fetches them from the hard drive. It also allows for installing programs on the hardware, ensuring the files are in the right places, and helps the processor to multi-task by having two programs open at once and switching between the processes quickly so it is not actually multi-tasking but looks like it is.

Without the OS, you would need to communicate directly with the hardware. This would probably mean communicating using machine code, or assembly language, which is very difficult and time-consuming, and no one would use computers.

ⓔ This student has covered both sections of the question, explaining the need for the OS in the third paragraph and describing several functions in the first two. The answer is suitably structured and covers both sections appropriately. This is a Level 3 response. **8 marks**

Question 8
Student B

(a) There are lots of different utility programs that come with your computer; utility programs are housekeeping programs. These include defragmentation, anti-virus, automatic updating and compressing.

ⓔ This student has given the names of four different utility programs, all of which are correct, but the first was already given in the question. The question only needed two. The question asked for a description of these; the student describes utility programs, but not the examples. **2 marks**

(b) Computers don't work without an OS, you wouldn't be able to do anything. It manages the memory, the hardware and the software, so you don't have to. There are lots of different OSs, like Windows, IOS and Linux, and they all work on different computers and do different things. Windows has images and buttons while Linux is text-based. The OS lets you log in by giving you a username and password and stops other people accessing your files.

ⓔ This student has named several features of an OS and given a description of one of these, but the others are lacking descriptions of what they do. They have briefly stated the need for an OS, but this needs further explanation. The answer covers both elements, but is very one-sided, therefore this a Level 2 response. **4 marks**

Question 8 mark scheme

(a) 1 mark for each utility program and 1 mark for its description. The answers given here are examples; other valid answers can also be accepted.
- Auto update.
- The latest versions of utilities/OS are downloaded without user intervention.

- System clean-up.
- Removes temp files/unused files.

- Disk check.
- Scans and resolves links between file fragments/disk segments.

- Anti-malware/anti-virus.
- Removes/quarantines malware/viruses.

- Compression software.
- Reduces file size.

(b) **Level 3, 7–8 marks** The answer demonstrates a sustained explanation of why an OS is needed and the functions it performs. There is a logically structured explanation, including relevant points, and both the need for and function of an OS are covered.

Level 2, 4–6 marks The answer includes an explanation of the functions of an OS and the need for an OS. There is a logically structured explanation, although one part may be brief.

Level 1, 1–3 marks The answer includes either a description of the functions of an OS or the need for it.

The following are indicative examples and other points would also be valid:
- To manage the hardware, peripherals, input/output devices…
- …allows installation/compatibility/device drivers.
- To manage memory…
- …transfers data between memory locations, CPU/main memory/secondary storage.
- To manage applications/platform for applications…
- …allows for installation of software/compatibility.
- For security…
- …allows for user accounts/passwords/access rights.
- To manage processes…
- …controls the CPU processes/ensures data are sent to processor.
- To manage user interface…
- …provides a GUI/command line to let the user interact with the hardware.

Hints and tips
Look carefully at the question. There are two parts to it. Make sure you answer both of these and explain every point that you make.

Question 9
Student A

(a) ALU stands for arithmetic logic unit. This part of the processor performs all of the calculations (such as 1 + 2) and logical decisions (such as AND, = etc.).

The two roles of the ALU — arithmetic and logical decisions — are correct (2), and a suitable example for each is given (1). 3 marks

(b) The control unit sends signals that tell data where to go to, both within the CPU and within memory, e.g. between registers and RAM.

This student has identified that the CU sends signals to control data (1) and where these data are moved between (1). 2 marks

(c) The clock is a vital part of the processor; it decides how fast the computer is. Each clock 'tick' means that another signal can be sent, for example a new F–E cycle can start or take place. The faster the clock is, the faster the processes can be completed.

e **This student has identified that the clock determines when signals are sent (1), that the clock determines when F–E cycles start (1) and that the faster the clock, the faster the processor (1). 3 marks**

Question 9
Student B

(a) The ALU does arithmetic and logic like adding numbers together.

e **This student has stated what the A and L stand for, but has not described their functions sufficiently to gain these marks. A suitable example is given (1). 1 mark**

(b) The CU moves data through the CPU.

e **This student has identified that the control unit is involved in the movement of data (1), but not that it does this by sending control signals. 1 mark**

(c) The clock is the speed of the processor. The faster the clock goes, the faster your computer will run so it won't lag as much. Whenever the clock moves on to the next time, another signal can be sent in the CPU.

e **This student has identified that the faster the clock, the more processes take place per second (1), and has also described how the clock controls the timing of signals (1). 2 marks**

Question 9 mark scheme

(a) 1 mark for each of the following points:
- Performs the calculations.
- Performs logical decisions.
- e.g. addition/subtraction/comparison/>=.

(b) 1 mark for each of the following points:
- Send signals to control how data…
- …are moved through CPU/between memory locations.

(c) 3 marks from:
- Controls the timing of signals.
- Each instruction has a set number of clock cycles to be executed.
- F–E cycle is synchronised with clock cycles.
- The faster the clock, the more processes can take place per second.

2.3 Fundamentals of computer networks

Question 10
Student A

(a) A LAN is a local area network and is more suitable. This is because a LAN only exists over a small area; the business is only over a small area so this is suitable. In a LAN the business can have its own media, it does not need to use telephone lines or satellites to send the data, which means it has more control over the network as it is only for the business.

e This student has correctly identified that a LAN is more appropriate (1), saying that the network is only needed over a small area (1) and that the company can use its own media (1), before expanding this to explain that telephones lines etc. do not need to be used (1). The student has also said that there is more control over the network, but has already gained the maximum marks. **4 marks**

(b) The staff may have a wireless printer that uses Bluetooth, so they can send work documents from their computer to the printer to be printed. They may also use tablets and could transfer work documents that they have been working on on their tablet to their laptop.

e This student has correctly identified that a PAN could be used between a computer and printer (1) and stated the purpose (1). They have given a second example, from tablets to laptops (1), and stated that this could be to send work files (1). **4 marks**

(c) HTTPS — this stands for Hypertext Transfer Protocol Secure. It lets data be sent and received over the internet securely; you can look out for the padlock symbol on the URL bar. Data can be sent securely by encrypting them.

Email, e.g. SMTP and IMAP — this allows you to send (SMTP) and receive (IMAP) emails across the internet.

e This student has correctly identified HTTPS as a protocol (1), and stated that it lets data be sent securely over the internet (1) using encryption (1). They have has given a second example, e-mail/SMTP/IMAP (1), and identified that SMTP is usually used to send emails (1) and IMAP to receive them (1). **6 marks**

Question 10
Student B

(a) LAN. LANs are over a small area, but WANs are only for large areas which this business isn't.

e This student has correctly identified that a LAN should be used (1), and that this is because it is only over a small area (1). Students should make sure that they check the number of marks available in a question, as this was worth 3 for the explanation, so further points needed to be made. **2 marks**

(b) They can connect their phones to the printer, so they can print things like photos. They can do the same thing with their phones to each other's phones.

e **This student has correctly identified that a phone could be connected to a printer (1) and that this can be used to print photos (1). They have also identified that phones can connect to each other (1), but have not identified what the PAN in this case is used for. 3 marks**

(c) Two protocols are HTTP and HTTPS. HTTP stands for Hypertext Transfer Protocol. It is used to send data on the internet. HTTPS has Secure on the end because data are sent safely so they can't be hacked.

e **This student has correctly identified two protocols, HTTP (1) and HTTPS (1). They have explained that HTTP sends data on the internet (1) and that HTTPS sends them securely (1). These answers needed to be explained further to gain the final marks. 4 marks**

Question 10 mark scheme

(a) 1 mark for LAN, max. 3 marks for the explanation from the following:
- Located over a small geographical area.
- Can use dedicated lines…
- …does not need to connect/rent external media e.g. telephone.
- Owns hardware used to communicate…
- …gives control over the network.
- Shared resources.
- Shared software licences.
- Can store information centrally.
- Lower error rates than WAN's due to dedicated communication links.

(b) 2 marks for each example, to max. 4. Accept any suitable example. The reason must be different for each. For example:
- Computer/laptop to printer…
- …to send documents for printing.
- Laptop to phone…
- …to send documents.
- Phone to phone…
- …to send images/documents.

(c) 1 mark for each protocol (max. two protocols), max. 3 marks for each. For example:
- HTTP (Hypertext Transfer Protocol).
- Identifies how data are communicated on WWW.
- Uses hyperlinks to link connect pages.

- HTTPS (Hypertext Transfer Protocol Secure).
- Allows for secure communication over network/internet.
- Authenticates the website/uses encryption.

- UDP (User Datagram Protocol).
- Part of IP (Internet Protocol).
- Used for sending packets over the internet.

- FTP (File Transfer Protocol).
- Used to transfer files between two computers.
- Can encrypt content for security.

- Email protocol.
- SMTP used for sending messages.
- IMAP used for receiving messages.

Question 11
Student A

(a) A protocol is a set of rules, for example deciding the speed to transmit data.

e **This is the correct definition. 1 mark**

(b) Two email protocols are IMAP and SMTP

e **These two protocols are correct. 2 marks**

(c)

Application
Transport
Internet
Network interface

e **This student has correctly given each layer name and both are in the correct place. 2 marks**

(d) The transport layer lets two devices agree how they are going to send data, so they are sending it at the same speed, in the same language and using the same packet size.

e **This student has correctly identified that it sets up the communication (1) and has given several examples of what is agreed (1). 2 marks**

(e) IP addresses identify all computers that are on the internet. They all have different IP addresses, a bit like people's addresses. When you enter a URL, the computer sends it to a DNS that has a table of URLs and IPs. It searches for the URL, finds it and gets the IP of the server storing the website. The computer sends the request to that IP, along with its own IP so it knows where to return the data to, and then the server sends the website back.

e **This student has identified an IP as being the unique address (1), that the URL goes to the DNS (1) which then finds the IP (1). They have described how the request is sent to the IP (1). The student has also said that the server then returns the website but has already gained the maximum marks. 4 marks**

Question 11
Student B

(a) Rules that are agreed.

e This is a simpler definition, but nevertheless valid. **1 mark**

(b) SMTP and Hotmail.

e SMTP is correct (1), but Hotmail is a brand name, not a protocol. **1 mark**

(c)

| Application |
| Transport |
| **Network** |
| **Internet** |

e This student has correctly put network in the first space (1). The second answer would be an alternative for the third layer, so it is incorrect here. **1 mark**

(d) It decides how the data will be transmitted, for example what language the two devices will use.

e This student's explanation of 'how the data will be transmitted' is not specific enough to gain the mark. The example is correct (1). **1 mark**

(e) An IP is a unique address. When you type a URL in, it doesn't go to the URL, it goes to the IP where the website is, and the website sends these data back to your IP.

e This student has identified an IP as a unique address (1), that the request is sent to the IP (1) and that the data for the website is returned (1), but did not explain how the IP was generated from the URL. **3 marks**

Question 11 mark scheme

(a) 1 mark for a set of rules (to govern communication between two devices).

(b) 1 mark for each protocol:
- SMTP/Simple Mail Transfer Protocol.
- IMAP/Internet Message Access Protocol

(c) 1 mark for each layer.

G	Application
C	Transport
A	**Network/internet**
E	**Data link/network interface**

(d) 1 mark for the purpose and 1 mark for an example. For example:
- Sets up communication between two devices.
- e.g. packet size, language.

(e) 4 marks from:
- URL is sent to DNS/domain name server.
- DNS finds IP.
- Request is sent to the IP…
- …for the computer/server storing the website.
- IP is a unique address for every device connected to the internet.
- Server sends the website data back to the IP the request came from.

2.4 Fundamentals of cyber security

Question 12
Student A

(a) There are lots of threats to networks, such as hackers and viruses that can damage your computer and data. Cyber security is the tools and software that you use to protect your computer and your network from these threats.

e **This student has identified that cyber security is the technology to protect your network (1) and described the potential threats it is protected against (1). 2 marks**

(b) One threat is from customers who have weak passwords. Passwords should be strong, i.e. more than eight characters, with capitals, lowercase and other symbols. If a customer's date of birth is used then it is quite easy to guess, and someone else can log into their account and steal their money.

A second threat is social engineering such as phishing and pharming. Social engineering means trying to manipulate people or trick them into giving you information. You might go to a website that you think belongs to the bank, but you have been redirected to a fake website, where you enter your details and then a fraudster has access to your bank account and they can steal your information.

e **Two different threats are identified correctly (2) and a description of each is given (2). Appropriate examples related to the bank are given (2) and the risk that this poses to the people involved is explained (2). 8 marks**

(c) The external company will attempt to gain access to the bank's website to find any weaknesses in the security of the website. There are two types of penetration testing, white-box and black-box, and both of these can be used on the bank's website. The white-box testing is used to pretend that they are an employee of the bank, who already has some access rights like usernames and passwords, and then they try and access more information like stealing money. Black-box is when they pretend to have no information at all and try and gain access to customers' accounts through the website.

e **This student has explained that the company will attempt to gain access to the website (1) and that they are trying to find security weaknesses (1). They have correctly given the names of two types of penetration testing (2) and explained each (2). 6 marks**

(d) One method is to use email confirmation. When the user requests to reset their password, the system sends an email to the registered email address. The customer has to click on this link as only the customer should be able to access their email.

A second method would be to use CAPTCHA. When you request to set up a new account, the website displays a message or code that a computer can't read, then the person has to read and enter this information to prove they are real.

e **Two different methods of authentication are given (2) and, a description of each (2). The student has explained how each would be used in this scenario (2). 6 marks**

Question 12
Student B

(a) Cyber security stops hackers getting into your computer.

e **This student has identified that it protects from a threat (1), but has not fully explained what it actually is, i.e. the technology, software, rules. 1 mark**

(b) Taking data into work on CDs and memory sticks is a threat because they could contain a virus that destroys the bank's data and all the customers will lose their money.

Shoulder surfing is when someone stands behind your shoulder and watches as you type in your PIN at an ATM. They then steal your bank card and take your money.

e **This student has given a description of the threat of removable media (1) and explained what could happen (1) with a relevant example (1). The second threat gives an example (1) and relates it to the bank (1). 5 marks**

(c) Penetration testing lets people try and hack the bank's website. They don't know how to gain access and they try and find a way in to steal people's money.

e **This student has explained that penetration testing is about attempting to gain access to the website (1) and that they don't have any knowledge e.g. usernames (1), but needed to explain further about the methods that are used. 2 marks**

(d) When you sign up on a website, an email is sent to your inbox and you have to click on the link to show that you are who you say you are.

e **Email authentication is described (1) and the reason for it is given although not explained well (1). The question asked for two methods, but the student has given only one. 2 marks**

Question 12 mark scheme

(a) 1 mark for each of the following points:
- Processes/actions/technology used to protect networks…
- …from attack/damage/unauthorised access.

(b) 1 mark for identifying the threat, 1 mark for a description, 2 marks for the risk to bank's data with an example. Max. 4 marks for each identified threat (max. two threats). For example:
- Threat: social engineering techniques.
- Description: manipulating people to give away confidential information.
- Example: phishing, pharming, shoulder surfing, blagging.
- Risk: customer could receive a fake email that says it is from the bank and they give away their account/PIN details.

- Threat: weak passwords.
- Description: description of secure password/insecure password.
- Example: someone can guess the password and log into people's accounts.
- Risk: access customers' accounts and transfer money.

- Threat: removable media.
- Description: devices used elsewhere may have a virus that can be transferred onto the network.
- Example: employee brings in work documents on a memory stick.
- Risk: the memory stick contains a virus that deletes data from the bank.

(c) 1 mark for the explanation: Penetration testing is when you try to get access to resources without knowing the usernames and passwords or using other normal methods of access. Examples must be related to the bank. 4 marks from:
- The company will attempt to gain access to the bank's website…
- …without knowledge of usernames, passwords etc.
- Attempt to find loopholes/security weaknesses.
- White-box testing…
- …e.g. pretend to be a bank employee who has some permissions/access.
- Black-box testing…
- …e.g. simulate an external attack such as from a hacker.

(d) Max. 3 marks for each method (max. two methods). For example:
- Email authentication.
- Sends an email link to reset the password to the user's email account.
- Ensures only a person can set up an account.

- CAPTCHA.
- Generates alphanumeric sequence that has to be entered.
- Ensures that it is a person setting up the account.

- Biometric security.
- Fingerprint recognition/retina scanner.
- Checks that it is the user who is requesting the password reset.

Question 13
Student A

(a) Virus ●
    Hacker ○
    Pharming ○
    Trojan ●
    Phishing ○

e Both pieces of malware are correctly identified. **2 marks**

(b) Spyware

e This is correct. **1 mark**

Question 13
Student B

(a) Virus ●
    Hacker ○
    Pharming ●
    Trojan ○
    Phishing ○

e Virus is correctly identified as a piece of malware (1). Pharming is an action carried out by a person, not a piece of software that can cause damage to your computer. **1 mark**

(b) Virus

e The question asked for one additional piece of malware; virus was given in part (a). No mark is awarded.

Question 13 mark scheme

(a) 1 mark for each correctly shaded lozenge. Minus 1 mark for each additional lozenge shaded.

Virus ●
Hacker ○
Pharming ○
Trojan ●
Phishing ○

(b) 1 mark for any appropriate name or type of malware. For example: worm, adware, spyware.

2.5 Ethical, legal and environmental impacts of digital technology

Question 14
Student A

Technology has reduced significantly in size and people are wearing technology that is discreet and easily hidden, such as smart watches. These devices give you access to your data, or devices, without actually having to take the devices out, so instead of walking around with your head down checking your phone, your watch can display everything you need. If someone makes a phone call, you can accept or reject it on your watch, instead of having to get your phone out. However, this increases the obsession with technology because people are spending so much of their time on computers and their phones that they are no longer socialising or interacting with people. Such technology may decrease social interaction even more, making people socially isolated.

Legally, people may have concerns over privacy, for example people can now wear cameras and walk around recording what people are doing without their permission or without people even knowing sometimes. In some circumstances, for some people like the police and ambulance workers, they can be very useful and life-saving, such as recording what they are doing when people commit crimes or attack them, and people can see exactly what happened instead of relying on what people say.

Some people may buy these devices because they are just the latest craze. They buy them and use them for a short time, then put them on one side along with other devices. These devices took energy and resources to build and then they just end up being thrown away. However, these newer devices are smaller, so they use fewer resources than buying a new larger one.

> ⓔ **This is a structured response to the question, covering the social, legal and environmental impacts of wearable technology, with advantages and disadvantages given for each area. This is a Level 3 response. 9 marks**

Question 14
Student B

Wearable technology is great because it's smaller and lets you record what you're doing, like using small cameras, and then you can post it online. Some people may try and use it to cheat in exams, though, by having information on their watches so when they check what the time is they get information, but these are usually banned in exams. Devices are making people less social because they spend all day on their phones using Snapchat and things to talk to people, rather than talking to them themselves, but this is also good because you can tell people who aren't with you what you're doing.

> ⓔ **This student has described several social impacts of wearable technology, including advantages and disadvantages. This is a Level 2 response because only social impacts are covered. 5 marks**

Question 14 mark scheme

Level 3, 7–9 marks There is a logically structured discussion of the advantages and disadvantages associated with the use of wearable technologies, including relevant points covering at least two of legal, social and environmental issues.

Level 2, 5–6 marks There is a logically structured discussion of the advantages and disadvantages associated with the use of wearable technologies, including at least two relevant points related to legal, social and environmental issues.

Level 1, 1–3 marks The answer includes advantages or disadvantages associated with the use of wearable technologies.

Guidance — indicative response

Advantages:
- Access information anywhere.
- Immediate response and interaction.
- Be mobile while using technology (instead of staying in front of computer).
- More discreet, e.g. hidden, can notify you when needed rather than staying connected.
- Monitor health, report to healthcare professionals.

Disadvantages:
- Reduced privacy/privacy concerns.
- Taking work home — cannot disconnect from technology.
- Constantly online — disengaging from society.
- More technology — takes energy to create and run, is it actually needed in addition to other devices.

Hints and tips

Look carefully at what the question is asking for (advantages and disadvantages), and make sure you cover both evenly. The question is interested in legal, social and environmental impacts, so make sure you give at least one point for each of these three areas.

THE ASSESSMENT OBJECTIVES (AOs)

These are used when writing exam papers to ensure there is an even coverage of skills. They determine what you are being asked to do and what key word is being used in the question.

Assessment objective descriptors

Assessment objective	Description
AO1	Demonstrate knowledge and understanding of the key concepts and principles of computer science. This will involve recalling definitions and key words, and demonstrating an understanding of what the theory topics are about. You may be asked to define, state, describe, explain etc.
AO2	Apply knowledge and understanding of key concepts and principles of computer science. This will involve using your knowledge to show your understanding, or applying it to a specific context, e.g. you may be given a scenario and asked to explain how something may be used in it, or why.
AO3	Analyse problems in computational terms: • to make reasoned judgements; and • to design, program, evaluate and refine solutions This could involve writing algorithms, pseudo-code and flowcharts. You may be asked to edit a program, evaluate it or improve it. You could also be asked to make a judgement (a decision) about how suitable something is, or is not, for a specific situation.

Assessment objective weightings

Paper 1 has most of its marks in the AO2 band, which means you will need to apply your knowledge. There are also a reasonable percentage of AO3 marks, so you may be asked to write and edit short programs. There are a few AO1s, so there may be some knowledge and concepts that you need to recall and explain.

Paper 2 does not have any AO3 marks, which means you will not be asked to write programs in this exam. Most of its marks are in AO1, which involves recalling, describing and explaining concepts, with the rest being AO2 marks, so you will have to apply your knowledge quite often in this exam.

The assessment objectives (AOs)

The **non-exam assessment** does not have any AO1 marks and few AO2s, so you will be applying some of your knowledge but you are not expected to recall, define or describe concepts. Most of the marks are for AO3 because you will be using computational thinking skills to produce a program and then to test it.

Breakdown of assessment objectives for GCSE

Component	AO1	AO2	AO3	Total
Paper 1	6%	22.5%	11.5%	40%
Paper 2	24%	16%	0%	40%
Non-exam assessment	0%	1.5%	18.5%	20%
Total	**30%**	**40%**	**30%**	**100%**